Bony Fish

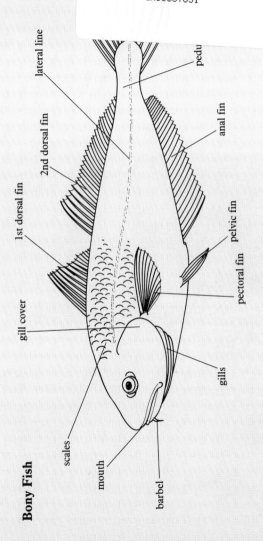

lateral line

pedu

anal fin

2nd dorsal fin

pelvic fin

1st dorsal fin

pectoral fin

gill cover

gills

scales

mouth

barbel

LETTS POCKET GUIDE TO

SEA & SEASHORE LIFE

The most common species of
European fish and other marine life
described and illustrated in colour

Pamela Forey and Cecilia Fitzsimons

CHARLES LETTS
Letts
of London®
FOUNDED 1796

CAUTION

The sea is beautiful and fascinating, but it can be dangerous and should always be treated with respect. When exploring at low tide, never let the incoming tide cut off your route back to the shore. Watch out for large waves which could sweep you off slippery rocks. Never try to walk on the mud of muddy shores, estuaries or saltmarshes; the mud can be soft and deep and you could be trapped in it. Always keep an eye on young children when they are near water.

If you turn a stone over on the shore, make sure you put it back the same way up. Otherwise the animals that were living on its underside will die.

This edition first published in 1994
by Charles Letts & Co Ltd
Letts of London House,
Parkgate Road,
London SW11 4NQ

'Letts' is a registered trademark of
Charles Letts & Co Limited

This edition produced by
Malcolm Saunders Publishing Ltd, London

© 1994 Malcolm Saunders Publishing Ltd

A CIP catalogue record for this book is available from the British Library

ISBN 1 85238 448 4

Printed in Spain

Contents

Introduction

The seas and oceans of our planet are home to some of the most fascinating creatures that live on Earth. This book is designed as an introduction to the rich underwater world of the seas around Europe and to life on their shores. We cannot hope to include all the species present in a book this size, so we have focused on marine fishes and the more obvious other sea creatures. The aim of the book is to enable you to identify fishes and other sea creatures that you may find on a beach, in an aquarium or even in a fishmonger's shop. And to give you some idea of how and where they live. Sea birds and marine mammals are described in the companion books in this series (**Birds** and **Mammals**) and so we have omitted them to make space for other creatures not included elsewhere. **Seashells** (another companion book in the series) provides a much more extensive description of the shells of Molluscs.

How to use this book

Several groups of animals and one group of plants are included in the book and it has been divided into eight sections to reflect this diversity. The sections are **Fishes**; **Echinoderms**; **Crustaceans**; **Molluscs**; **Segmented Worms**; **Coelenterates**; **Other Animals**; and **Seaweeds**. Each section is indicated by a different colour band at the top of the page (see Contents Page). To identify your animal or plant, first read through the information in the *Guide to Identification* and then turn to the relevant page.

Guide to Identification

First decide to which section your organism belongs by reading the following descriptions.

 FISHES are probably the most familiar of the animals of the sea and almost need no description. The majority have the classic, streamlined fish shape, but even the few that do not (like seahorses or eels) still have the other fishy features — fins on back and belly, paired pectoral and pelvic fins, and a vertical tail fin. They breathe by means of gills.

Fishes can be split into two great groups. The first is **Sharks** and **Rays** (pp.16–25); although sharks and rays appear to be so different they are actually much more closely related to each other than to any other fishes; and they have many features in common. These include:

8

gills open to the water through a series of gill-slits behind the head; mouth on the underside of the head; body covered in a thick skin with heavy, tooth-like scales embedded in it; and skeleton formed of cartilage. Sharks have the typical streamlined shape of many open sea fishes. Rays are flattened from top to bottom, to lie hidden on the seabed.

The second group is the **Bony Fishes** (pp.26–70), so-called because their skeleton is formed of bone. These fishes have their gills covered by a gill cover behind the head; the mouth at or near the point of the head; and the body usually covered in relatively fragile, loose scales. They vary in shape enormously, from the open ocean fishes with the classic shape of tunny and cod, to the flatfishes that live on the bottom, to the odd shapes of seahorses and eels. (Flatfishes actually lie on their sides, so that the upper side appears to be the back.)

Lampreys and **hagfishes** (p.71) are eel-like animals that look like fishes (especially like eels) but are really not fishes at all. They lack jaws, have no paired pectoral or pelvic fins and have no scales. They are included in the fish section here for convenience.

ECHINODERMS (pp.72–75) are found only in the sea, not on land or in fresh water. They are unique in many ways. For one thing they are generally radially or pentamerously symmetrical (most animals are bilaterally symmetrical), with a mouth in the centre of one side of the body, and anus at the centre on the other side; they have a unique hydraulic system used for walking and feeding, the most obvious part of which are the rows of radially arranged tube feet. They have a skeleton formed of many interlocking plates, often with spines and pincers on it.

They include the sea urchins, starfishes, brittlestars and sea-cucumbers. Sea-cucumbers are rather different from the others, and can be understood as an elongated, spineless sea-urchin laid on its side.

CRUSTACEANS (pp.76–85) are jointed-legged animals. Their bodies are covered in a hard but (relatively) flexible exoskeleton and are formed of many segments. Some crustaceans have bodies formed of many similar segments; others have bodies with three distinct sections, the head, thorax and abdomen. All have jointed legs.

They include the familiar crabs, lobsters and prawns, but also the less familiar sandhoppers and others. Barnacles belong here, even though they appear to be more like limpets at first glance; under water they open up and reveal their jointed legs.

MOLLUSCS are a large group of animals which include (among others) snails, winkles, slugs, cockles, mussels, chitons, squid and octopus.

Gastropod Molluscs (pp.87–92) are familiar as snails and slugs. Snails have a soft, unsegmented body covered by a calcareous shell, coiled in the most familiar forms, like garden snails. However, the shells of marine snails are more variable; some, like limpets, have simple conical shells while others, like cowries, have the coils tucked inside the shell. When the animals emerge from their shells, they have the same gliding foot, and head with tentacles as their land cousins (see also tube-worms on p.105; some of them have tubes which resemble the shells of gastropod snails; and barnacles on p.85, which resemble limpets).

Sea-slugs (p.92) are much more beautiful than land slugs, often brightly coloured with gills and tentacles on their backs; but they are basically shell-less snails like their terrestrial cousins, with a gliding foot and tentacled head.

Chitons (p.86) are also molluscs, with a superficial resemblance to limpets. But they are not gastropods. And can be immediately recognized by the series of articulated, calcareous plates that cover their backs.

Bivalve Molluscs (pp.93–99) are very different to other molluscs at first glance; however, internally they share many biological features with Gastropods and others. Most bivalves can be very quickly recognized from their shell, which is divided into two more or less equal valves. They include mussels, scallops, razor shells and many others. Shipworms (p.99) belong here (even though at first glance they look more like worms; their much reduced bivalve shell can be seen at one end of the body).

Squids, Cuttlefish and **Octopus** (pp.100–102) are also molluscs. They have no visible shells and have torpedo-like or bag-like bodies, with large eyes and a foot divided into eight tentacles (squid and cuttlefish have two arms as well). The shell (when present) is now inside the body.

SEGMENTED WORMS (pp.103–107) have long, worm-like bodies divided into many similar, more or less bristly segments. Some of them (the Errant Worms, like Ragworms) have distinct heads, often with tentacles, and they crawl around on shores and among rocks. Tube Worms live in tubes and often have a crown of tentacles on the head; this is the part which is visible when the worm emerges from its tube. Burrowing Worms live in burrows in sand or mud; many of these also have tentacles on their heads, while others, like Lugworms, resemble earthworms, with simple segmented bodies. (See also Shipworms on p.99, and Sea-cucumbers on p.75.)

COELENTERATES (pp.108–112) is the biological name given to the group which includes sea anemones, corals and jellyfish. They are generally soft-bodied, flower-like animals, with a bag-like body and a mouth at one end; there are often ring(s) of tentacles around the mouth. Many of them live in colonies which at first glance look like one animal; in fact each colony consists of many individual animals (called polyps) living together.

Anemones have soft columnar bodies with a crown of tentacles. Jellyfish have bodies like soft umbrellas fringed with tentacles; they float in the sea (like the Portuguese Man-o'-war which also belongs here and which resembles little else). Corals are not found to any great extent in European waters but soft corals are. Both are colonial coelenterates which form shells with many holes; the soft flower-like polyps live in the holes; corals form hard shells; soft corals form flexible ones (see also Sponges on p.115; and Sea-squirts on p.113).

 In the final animal section are three unrelated groups of animals: **SPONGES, SEA-SQUIRTS** and **SEA-MATS**. They are simple animals which might almost be mistaken for plants because they do not move about. Or they may not look like living organisms at all. Sponges and sea-squirts may be simple bag-like animals, sponges with a single opening at the top, sea-squirts with two siphon-like openings near the top; or they may form encrustations on rocks and seaweeds. Sea-mats always form encrustations on rocks or seaweeds; they have a distinctive compartmentalized structure. For more information on these groups, turn to the relevant pages: Sponges p.115, Sea-mats p.114, Sea-squirts p.113. (See also soft corals on p.112; and red seaweeds on p.121.)

 SEAWEEDS are the one group of plants included in this book. They are mostly simple, frond-like plants, formed of a branched or simple blade, attached to the rocks by a holdfast. The three groups of seaweeds included here are Green, Brown and Red Seaweeds.

Green Seaweeds (p.116) are usually bright green in colour and are often found where fresh water runs into the sea.

Brown Seaweeds (pp.117–119) are generally brown in colour and are the most obvious on the shore; wracks cover the rocks on the middle shore, kelps on the lower shore. They are responsible for the distinctive zones observed on many of the Atlantic seashores.

Red Seaweeds (pp.120–121) are generally red or reddish-brown; they are more sensitive to bright light than the other two groups, and so are found further down the shore, in shady pools or under other seaweeds; and into deeper water than the other two. Some of the reds are calcified; these may form crystalline fringes in rock pools or flat encrustations on rocks.

What's on a Page

Once you have decided to which group your organism belongs, turn to the pages on which representative species of that group are described and illustrated. Compare the information on the relevant pages to make a positive identification.

In the fish section, you will find one fish on each page (perhaps with an illustration of a related species that is described in box four). In the other sections, many of the pages are devoted to groups of animals rather than to individual species. For instance we have included a page on starfishes; by making this a group page we can give you some idea of the range of starfishes found in European waters, even in our limited space.

On each page you will find the Common name and Latin name of the species or group at the top. The length of the animal is also given. Four boxes provide information about the species or group illustrated. The first box provides details of features or combinations of features, which together with the illustration, make identification possible. The second and third boxes provide information on habitat and biology, what sort of places they are found in, what they feed on. If they nip, bite or sting, a warning symbol has been included in the illustration. (NB. Some animals that bite or sting are quite dangerous, therefore they should be treated with caution.)

Warning Symbol

 This animal may nip, bite or sting.

The third box provides information on the distribution of the species group. An indication is also given here if a species is commercially important. The fourth box gives information about the members of a group if this is a group page; or about related or similar species. On some pages related species are also illustrated.

Also scattered throughout the book are pages of Other Common Species. These provide additional information on less common or less widely distributed species which are nevertheless of interest.

Specimen Page

Latin name

Colour band denotes group of animals (or plants)

Name of animal

Symbol of group

Length of animal

Warning symbol

Colour illustration

♂ Male

♀ Female

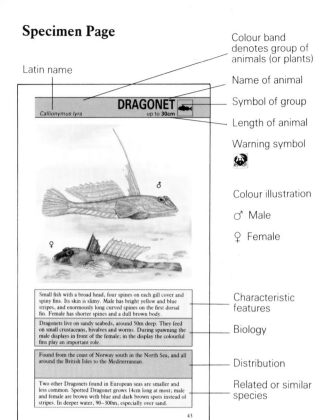

DRAGONET

Callionymus lyra   up to **30cm**

♂

♀

Small fish with a broad head, four spines on each gill cover and spiny fins. Its skin is slimy. Male has bright yellow and blue stripes, and enormously long curved spines on the first dorsal fin. Female has shorter spines and a dull brown body.

Characteristic features

Dragonets live on sandy seabeds, around 50m deep. They feed on small crustaceans, bivalves and worms. During spawning the male displays in front of the female; in the display the colourful fins play an important role.

Biology

Found from the coast of Norway south in the North Sea, and all around the British Isles to the Mediterranean.

Distribution

Two other Dragonets found in European seas are smaller and less common. Spotted Dragonet grows 14cm long at most; male and female are brown with blue and dark brown spots instead of stripes. In deeper water, 90–300m, especially over sand.

Related or similar species

43

Where do marine animals and plants live?

Marine animals and plants (like their terrestrial cousins) are often quite specific about where they will live. Some animals live in shallow coastal waters, others in the open sea; some swim in the upper layers of the sea, others live on the seabed; some live buried in mud, others attached to rocks or crawling around among seaweeds. On the shore some species live in muddy estuaries, others on exposed rocky shores, yet others on sandy beaches; they may live at high, mid or low tide levels. The information in boxes two and three will help you to look for animals in appropriate places and to identify them accurately.

Many of the animals in this book live in water too deep for easy access. So it may be difficult for you to see them in the wild. However many of the fishes can be caught by angling. Those caught commercially can often be seen at your local fishmonger's shop. And many seaside towns have marine aquaria.

If you want to see marine animals and plants in the wild, the easiest place to look is on the shore, especially on the Atlantic and North Sea shores. The Mediterranean shores are much less rich in wildlife since the Mediterranean does not have tides.

The effects of tides

Tides come in and go out roughly twice a day. This means there are two high tides and two low tides every 24 hours, with each day's tides about one hour later than the previous day's. Spring tides are the highest and lowest and occur every two weeks near the full or new moon. Neap tides are the least extreme and occur at fortnightly intervals between the spring tides. Because of the tides, it is possible to recognize a series of zones on a seashore (see illustration). They are as follows:

Splash Zone. Zone above the extreme high water of spring tides. It is still regularly drenched by spray at high tide.

Upper Shore. The zone above average high tide level, uncovered for much of the time, only covered by the sea at high tide as the tides approach their spring highs.

Middle Shore. The wide zone between the average high tide level and the average low tide level; covered and uncovered by the sea twice daily for much of the time.

Lower Shore. The narrow zone extending from average low tide level to extreme low water of spring tides. This level is only uncovered when the tides approach their spring lows.

Subtidal Level. Shallow water below extreme spring low tide level. This zone is never uncovered but is subject to higher fluctuations of temperature and salinity than the open sea.

Tidal Levels and Zonation

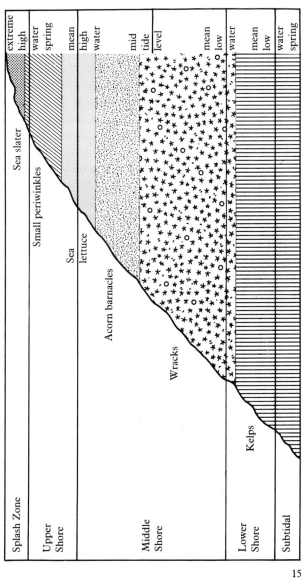

An enormous shark with a floppy dorsal fin. Very long gill slits run around the 'neck' from the back to under the throat. Its teeth are minute. It varies from grey-brown to nearly black in colour, becoming paler beneath.

A harmless creature despite its great size. It swims slowly through the water with its mouth open, using the stiff, bristle-like gill rakers on the insides of the gill slits as a filter for catching plankton. Females give birth to live young.

A mainly oceanic shark, found across the Atlantic and the Mediterranean, seen off the coasts in summer. It swims in shoals in the open ocean, singly near the coast.

No similar species when full grown. The long gill slits distinguish young individuals from any other shark. Full grown individuals can be distinguished from whales by their gill slits and vertical tail fins.

BLUE SHARK

Prionace glauca   up to **3.8m**

1

A large shark, deep indigo blue on the back with a white belly. It has a long pointed snout, distinctively long, curved pectoral fins and a curved upper lobe to the tail. One of the few dangerous sharks in European waters.

Blue Sharks are often accompanied by **Pilot Fish** (**1**). They hunt pelagic fishes like herring, whiting and mackerel; and may become tangled in the nets of boats fishing for these species. Females give birth to live young.

Normally found in open sea of the Atlantic and Mediterranean; they migrate inshore, eg. into the English Channel and Irish Sea in summer, but do not approach the coasts. Regarded as pests by commercial fishermen but a popular sport fish.

The Thresher is another large shark (up to 6m long), recognisable by its very long tail (as long as the body). It lives in the open ocean, coming inshore in summer, where it may 'round up' shoals of herring and other fishes with its tail.

A large, heavy-bodied shark with a rounded snout and a strong keel each side of the tail. Two dorsal fins, first much larger than second. Teeth large and triangular, with a cusp each side of the base. Dark blue or blue-grey above, pale cream beneath.

These sharks swim mainly near the surface where they hunt shoaling fishes like herring, mackerel, cod etc. Females bear live young.

Present in the Atlantic and Mediterranean throughout the year, adults approaching to within 16km of the coasts in summer, young ones close enough to be caught from the shore. Popular for sport fishing.

The related Mako swims in warmer waters of the Atlantic, infrequently migrating north to the British coast in summer. It is more streamlined, with a sharp snout; its first dorsal fin originates behind the pectoral fins; and its teeth lack cusps.

STARRY SMOOTH HOUND
Mustelus asterias   about **120cm**

A small, slender, rather sluggish shark, with smooth skin compared to other sharks. Its two dorsal fins are about the same size. Dull grey back, shading to light cream or grey belly, with small, star-like, white spots on back and sides.

Groups of these sharks swim together near the seabed. They have flat, slab-like teeth, which they use like a mill to grind up their food, mainly crabs and lobsters. Females give birth to live young.

Found in the North Sea and Atlantic, south to the Mediterranean, generally on the continental shelf in water down to 160m deep, migrating into shallower, coastal waters in summer. Often caught by fishermen from the shore.

The Smooth Hound is very similar but has no white spots; it has a similar lifestyle and distribution. However it is much less common.

SPURDOG
up to **120cm**

Squalus acanthias

A small, slender shark with a small, venomous spine in front of the dorsal fin; it can inflict a painful wound. No anal fin. All five gill openings are in front of the pectoral fins. Dark grey with rounded white spots on the back and sides.

Found in large moving shoals at all levels (these sharks are active swimmers) in inshore and offshore waters to a depth of 1000m. Feed on a large variety of prey, all sorts of fishes, squid, octopus, worms, crabs etc. Females bear live young.

Shoals of Spurdogs migrate unpredictably throughout the north Atlantic, North Sea and Mediterranean. A commercially important fish; sold as flake, rock eel or rock salmon.

One of the Spiny Sharks; they all have strong spines in front of the dorsal fin and no anal fin. 15 species occur in European waters. The Velvet Belly is another small member of this group (up to 50cm long); it has black, velvety skin.

LESSER SPOTTED DOGFISH
Sciliorhinus caniculus up to **75cm**

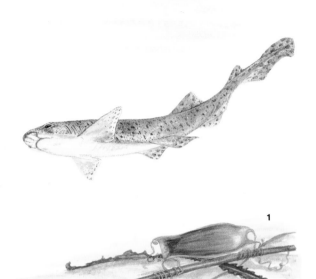

1

A small shark with a short rounded snout. Sandy brown with many dark brown spots on its back and sides, shading to cream beneath. Beneath the snout and overlying the front of the mouth is a large flap (formed of two joined nasal flaps).

Usually found over sandy or muddy seabeds, around sand banks. Feeds mostly on molluscs and crustaceans. Females lay their eggs in horny egg-cases known as **Mermaid's Purses** (**1**); these are often washed ashore.

The commonest European shark. Found in coastal waters of the north Atlantic and Mediterranean, at depths of 5–110m, mostly around 55m. Of considerable commercial value, sold as flake, rock eel or rock salmon. Also used for dissection.

Nurse Hound is similar but larger (up to 1.5m long), stouter and less common. It has two separate nasal flaps which do not overlie the front of the mouth. It is most common over rough, rocky seabeds, usually at 20–60m deep.

♀

A distinctive fish, like a flattened shark but not so flat as a ray. It has a broad head and large, wing-like pectoral fins. No anal fin. Spiracles are on the top of the head and larger than the eyes. Lower lobe of the tail is longer than the upper lobe.

A bottom-living fish, found half-buried in sand or gravel on the bottom, mostly at 5–7m deep in summer. Can also swim actively with wide sweeps of the tail. Feeds on flatfishes, rays, whelks, crabs etc. Females give birth to live young.

Found in deep water in winter, around the coast of the Mediterranean, Atlantic and eastern North Sea in summer, north to the Shetland Isles. Not the Monkfish tails sold in shops; these come from the **Angler**.

True sharks are more streamlined; the upper lobe of their tails is longer than the lower lobe. Rays are much more flattened. Two other Angelfish species are found in the Mediterranean and adjacent Atlantic.

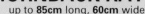

THORNBACK RAY

Raja clavata up to **85cm** long, **60cm** wide

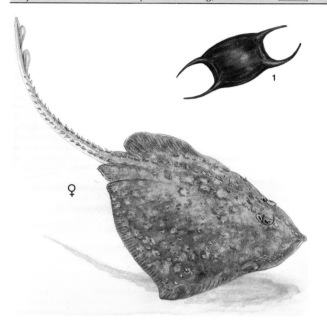

♀

Small ray with a short snout, marbled grey or fawn in colour, with coarse prickles on back and belly. Females and young have a row of spines on the back, males on tail only. Pectoral fins are sharply angled at the tips, with an angle of about 90°.

Lies on the seabed in mud, sand or gravel. Feeds on crustaceans like crabs and shrimps; it may also swim upwards and catch fish with its pectoral fins. Females lay eggs in horny egg-cases known as **Mermaid's Purses** (**1**); these are often washed ashore.

The most common ray in shallow inshore European waters. Found in water up to 60m deep, all along the Atlantic, North Sea and Mediterranean coasts and into the Black Sea. This is an important commercial fish; it is sold as skate.

Blonde Ray has more rounded pectoral fins and prickles on the back in adults; young are smooth-skinned. Its back is light brown with small black spots. Common to south and west of Britain in water less than 100m deep, especially over sand.

23

SKATE
up to **2m** long, **130cm** wide; up to **90kg**   *Raja batis*

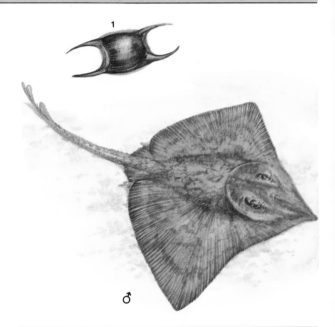

♂

A large ray with quite a long, pointed snout, prickles on the back (females on front part of back only), a line of spines down the tail and prickly underside. Back olive-grey or brown with light and dark spots, underside blue-grey with dark spots.

Found in water from 35–600m deep. Feeds on a variety of bottom-living fishes and crustaceans, also swimming upwards to catch other fishes. **Mermaid's Purse (1)** similar to that of Thornback Ray, but large (15–24cm long as opposed to 6cm).

The largest European ray and probably the most common deepwater ray in the North Sea and Atlantic. Found from northern Scandinavia to Spain and into the Mediterranean. An important commercial fish; sold as skate.

Long-nosed Skate has a very long snout. This is another large deep-water ray, found off the Atlantic coasts but not in the North Sea or Irish Sea. It is sold as skate in the shops.

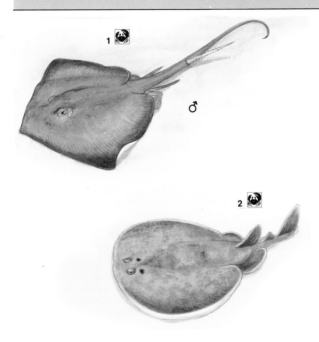

Sting Ray (1)

A large distinctive ray (up to 2.5m long) with an almost straight front edge (except for the pointed snout) & a long tail. There is a poison spine half-way along the tail; this can cause a nasty injury. No dorsal fins. Skin mostly smooth, with a few spines in large individuals. Back grey, olive or brown, creamy beneath with darker edges. Fairly common in shallow inshore waters & estuaries of Med., N. Sea & Atlantic, north to southern Scandinavia. Often buried in sand.

Electric Ray (2)

A large rounded ray (up to 1.8m long), with a short tail. It has two rounded dorsal fins, the first much larger than the second, & smooth skin. Dark brown, black or blue back, white beneath. Can deliver a powerful electric shock from electric organs on each side of the head, if handled incautiously; voltage depends on size of fish. Normally found in shallow water from 10–50m deep. From English Channel south to Med. & African coast, more common further south.

HALIBUT
over **2.5m**; up to **300kg**   *Hippoglossus hippoglossus*

1

An extremely large flatfish, with quite a long, narrow body, thick in cross-section. Mouth to right of eyes, jaws large. Lateral line strongly curved over pectoral fin. Tail fin concave. Dark olive green 'back', pearly white beneath.

Young fish live on offshore and coastal banks, older fish on the continental shelf edge. On sand, gravel and clay seabeds. They migrate long distances, staying in water around 3–5 °C. They prey on crustaceans, other fishes and molluscs.

North Atlantic from Norway across to Iceland, Greenland and North America. Also south around the western coast of the British Isles to the Bay of Biscay. A valuable food fish but over-fished and now rare in many areas where once found.

Dab (1) is similar in shape but small (up to 40cm long). Its tail is convex and its 'back' rough to the touch. Very common in coastal waters from the Bay of Biscay northwards. On sand banks and sandy shores, especially at depths of 20–40m.

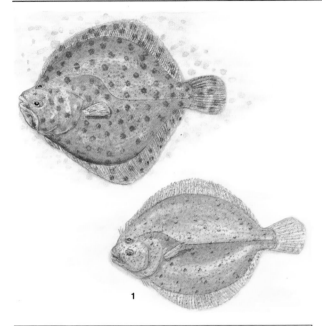

1

A large flatfish with an almost circular body, its 'back' coloured to match the seabed, white beneath; many bony tubercles cover the 'back'. Mouth is to left of eyes. Dorsal fin starts in front of the eyes. Jaws large, strongly curved.

Found on sand and gravel seabeds, from the shore to 80m deep (not in estuaries), younger fish nearer the shore. Very young fish may be seen on sandy beaches and in rock pools. Adults feed almost entirely on fishes, sand eels, pilchards, cod etc.

Found from the southern Baltic Sea into the Atlantic, through the North Sea and down the west coasts of the British Isles to the Mediterranean. This is very valuable food fish which commands a high price. Most are caught in the North Sea.

Brill (1) also has its mouth to the left of its eyes. Its oval body grows up to 60cm long. It has smooth scales rather than tubercles on its 'back'. Found in shallow water, on sand and gravel in the North Sea, Atlantic and Mediterranean.

27

PLAICE

Up to **90cm**; usual max **50cm**   *Pleuronectes platessa*

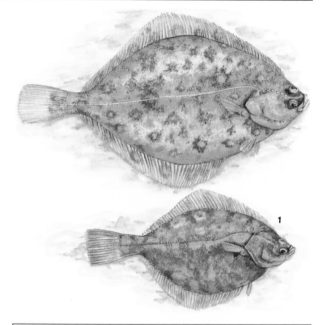

1

A distinctively coloured flatfish, brown on the upper side with bright red or orange spots. Underside white. Mouth small, terminal, to the right of the eyes. Skin smooth but 4–7 bony knobs run from the eyes to the start of the lateral line.

Found in inshore waters from about 3–120m deep, youngest fish nearest the shore. Most common on sand, also on mud and gravel. They feed mainly by day, more intensively in summer than in winter, catching crustaceans, molluscs and worms etc.

Found from the Baltic Sea and northern coast of Norway, around Iceland, south in the North Sea and along the western coasts of the British Isles to the western Mediterranean. Very important commercial flatfish and a good angling fish.

Flounder (**1**) grows up to 50cm long. It has toothed scales along bases of anal and dorsal fins, and along lateral line; with one or two bony knobs at start of lateral line. Found in estuaries and brackish water of North Sea, Atlantic and Mediterranean..

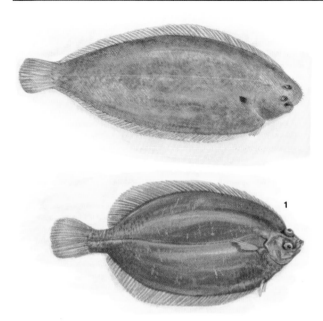

DOVER SOLE

Solea solea

up to **50cm**

A rather elongated flatfish, distinguished by the rounded head with dorsal fin extending onto front of head. Mouth is to right of eyes. Dorsal and anal fins are joined to tail fin. 'Back' dark brown with darker blotches; black spot on pectoral fin.

Common in inshore and offshore waters, from a few metres to 120m deep, shallower water in summer, deeper in winter. On sand and sandy mud, partly buried in bright light, active in dull weather and at night. Feeds on crustaceans, bivalves, worms.

Found from the southern coast of Scandinavia, in the North Sea and down the western coasts of the British Isles to the Mediterranean (rare north of Scotland). A valuable food fish, mostly trawled by night.

Lemon Sole (**1**) is more closely related to **Plaice** than to Dover Sole in spite of its name. It is smooth and slimy to touch. Found on coastal banks, especially on gravel, at depths of 40–200m in North Sea and northern Atlantic. A valuable food fish.

29

A distinctive fish, with a very broad head, wide open mouth and large curved teeth. Skin loose, scaleless and fringed with loose flaps, especially on the sides. Several spines on the head; the foremost has a fleshy flap on the tip (the lure).

Found mostly at depths of 20–550m or more, most often in deeper water. It lies partly buried in sand or mud on the seabed, leaving the lure exposed, angling for smaller fishes. It catches many kinds of fish, also lobsters, crabs and squid.

Found in the northern Atlantic from Norway to Iceland, south in the Atlantic and North Sea to the Mediterranean and the coast of Africa. Sold without head or skin, as monkfish tails.

No similar species.

A rounded, dark grey or blue-green fish, with bony, warty plates all over, and rows of spines on back and sides. Pelvic fins form a sucking disc beneath the head. Dorsal fin is near the tail. Males have an orange belly in the breeding season.

Found on seabeds from low-tide line to 300m deep, mostly down to 50m. Feeds on crustaceans, worms, fishes and molluscs. Females lay eggs on lower shore in northern areas of its range; males guard them. Larvae often drift on pieces of seaweed.

Found from the coast of Portugal north in the Atlantic and North Sea to the far north coast of Norway; also around Iceland and in the Arctic Ocean. It can be eaten smoked or salted. The roe is sold as cheap caviar.

No similar species.

JOHN DORY
up to **40cm**

Zeus faber

A deep-bodied fish, flattened from side to side with a very spiny first dorsal fin. Anal fin also spiny. Spines run along the belly and alongside dorsal and anal fins. Jaws massive. Yellow-brown or grey with a light-ringed spot on each side.

A solitary fish, found close inshore to a depth of 200m. Usually over a sandy seabed, often near rocks. It keeps station by undulating movements of its fins and stalks other fishes, suddenly snapping them up by protruding its massive jaws.

Found to the west and south of the British Isles, south to the coast of Africa and the Mediterranean. It may wander into the North Sea. An excellent food fish, eaten in France and southern Europe.

No similar species.

1

A large-headed fish, with strong spines on snout and gill covers. Spines also each side of the dorsal fin. Pectoral fins red on the outside, bright blue inside; their first three rays are quite separate. Body dull red with a yellow or white belly.

Found in loose shoals on the seabed, most often at depths of 50–150m, usually on sand or gravel. They grunt to each other and walk around on their pectoral fins which they also use to search for food. They eat shrimps, crabs, fishes and bivalves.

The largest gurnard in European waters. Quite common in the Irish Sea and Central North Sea, and south to the Mediterranean and Black Sea. Rare further north. A popular angling fish and good to eat.

Of six gurnard species in European waters, four are common. The most common, the **Grey Gurnard** (1) is found from shore-line to 140m deep in the Atlantic and Mediterranean, often in sandy coves and estuaries in summer. It grows up to 40cm long.

POGGE
up to **15cm**

Agonus cataphractus

A small fish covered with bony plates. It has a sharp spine on each gill cover and a pair of spines on the snout. The head is broad with many small barbels on the underside. Colour brown with broad darker bands (saddles) across the back; belly cream.

Very common in inshore waters and estuaries. Lives on the seabed, in water 5–200m deep, usually on sand or mud. Feeds on a variety of bottom-living animals, mostly crustaceans, also worms, molluscs etc.

Found on the coasts of Norway and Iceland, in the Western Baltic and North Sea, along the western coasts of the British Isles to the English Channel. All year round further north, but only in winter in the south.

No similar species.

BULL ROUT

Myxocephalus scorpius

up to **30cm**

Small, scaleless fish with broad spiny head, short spines on its gill covers, large spiny fins, and a row of spiny scutes on each side. The membrane from the gill covers extends into a flap under the throat. Colour brownish, varying with season.

A slow-moving fish which lives on sandy and muddy seabeds, from the shore to water 60m deep. Feeds on crustaceans and other fishes. Eggs deposited in rock crevices or among seaweeds. Spines can cause nasty cuts which can turn septic.

Found around the British Isles and north to the coast of Norway. In shallow water and on shore among seaweeds further north, in deeper water in the south. Can cause problems for commercial fishermen by eating shrimps, prawns and fish fry.

One of several Bullheads found on European coasts. Sea Scorpion is smaller (up to 15cm); the topmost of its gill cover spines is longer than the others. On rocky shores under seaweeds in Atlantic and North Sea, north from the Bay of Biscay.

A small fish with smooth, slimy skin and no scales. Long dorsal fin has a dip in the middle. Pelvic fin has only two long rays; it is placed under the throat. Colour of this fish varies with habitat; it is usually blotched in green and brown.

The most common fish on rocky shores; also found in sandy and muddy shores, mostly from mid-tide level downwards. It lives in pools, under stones and seaweeds. Browses on algae and barnacles, eating also any crustaceans or molluscs among them.

Found on the southwestern coast of Norway, on coasts all around the British Isles, and south to the southern coast of Portugal. Found in deeper water in winter. Eaten by seabirds.

Shanny is one of a group of fishes known as blennies. Most have a branched tentacle above each eye. Tompot Blenny (with such a tentacle) is a small yellowish fish, found over stony ground in water 6–8m deep, south from British Isles to the Mediterranean.

BUTTERFISH

Pholis gunnellus

up to **25cm**

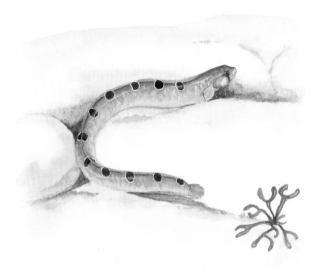

A small, elongated, very slimy fish with a long narrow dorsal fin. Brownish in colour with irregular darker brown bands and a dark stripe across each eye. There are about 12 round, black, white-ringed spots on either side of the dorsal fin.

Common on the seashore from mid-tide to low-tide level, beneath seaweeds, in rock pools and crevices; also in deeper waters to 30m deep. Feeds on crustaceans, worms and molluscs. Female lays her eggs under rocks and usually guards them.

Found on the coasts of Iceland and Norway, in the western Baltic, and north of the English Channel in the North Sea and Atlantic. An important food fish for other, commercially valuable fishes.

No similar species. Butterfish is related to the **Shanny** and other blennies.

FIVE-BEARDED ROCKLING
up to **20cm**
Ciliata mustela

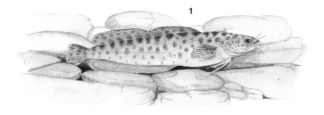

Small, dark red-brown, elongated fish with five barbels, one on the chin, four on the upper lip. Two dorsal fins; the first has a single large ray and a row of hair-like rays behind, the second is long and narrow like the anal.

An abundant fish in pools on rocky shores; also found in pools around rocks and breakwaters on sandy beaches, and on subtidal waters. They feed on a variety of crustaceans.

From the coasts of northern Norway, south on both coasts of the North Sea and western coasts of the British Isles to Portugal.

Other rocklings are found in offshore waters, like the **Three-bearded Rockling** (**1**). All have the distinctive dorsal fins and three to five barbels around the mouth; they vary in colour and distribution.

A small, elongated fish with a heavy head and thick lips. Two dorsal fins, both quite short; the second is similar to the anal. Pelvic fins are fused together into a weak sucking disc on the belly. Grey with a line of small spots along each side.

This is the most common goby of intertidal pools on sandy or muddy shores; it is often seen in estuaries or at the water's edge. In winter they migrate into deeper water. They feed on small crustaceans.

Found from the Baltic Sea, south along North Sea and Atlantic coasts to the Mediterranean. An important food fish for seabirds and other fishes.

Fifteen gobies live on European coasts; all have sucking discs. Painted Goby is brown with black spots; it lives in low-tide pools on rough shores and in eel-grass beds. **Black Goby** (**1**) grows 15cm long; it lives in estuaries and sheltered bays.

BALLAN WRASSE
up to **50cm**

Labrus bergylta

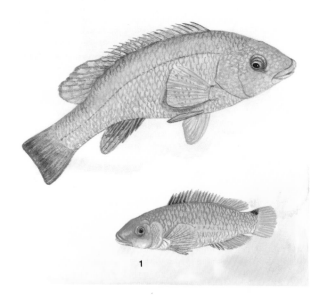

1

Deep-bodied, rather long fish. Single dorsal fin, front part spiny, rear part soft-rayed. Head heavy with thick lips. Colour varies; often green to green brown, belly and paired fins often reddish with white spots. Back edge of each scale dark.

Young fish are common in intertidal rock pools, older fish around offshore rocks into water 30m deep. Most often solitary or in twos and threes. They feed on prawns, crabs, squat lobsters, molluscs and barnacles, scraping them off the rocks.

Common from the western coast of Scotland south to the Canary Islands and in the Mediterranean, less common in the North Sea and around Scandinavian coast.

One of seven wrasse species found in European waters, all small inshore fishes. **Goldsinny** (**1**) is relatively common on steep, rocky, weed-covered Atlantic shores and in the Mediterranean. It grows 18cm long at most.

A reddish fish, with yellow stripes on dorsal fins and sides, two barbels under the chin, and two high, well-separated dorsal fins, the first with thin flexible spines. Scales large and fragile, often missing. Snout blunt, sloping steeply to mouth.

Found mainly on sandy or rocky seabeds, in coastal waters in summer, in deeper waters in winter, to a maximum depth of 50m. They feed on bottom-living animals, crustaceans, molluscs, worms and fishes, using their barbels to search for food.

Relatively common from the English Channel and Irish coast south to the Mediterranean; also more rarely in the North Sea. Excellent food fishes; commercially important in Mediterranean and southern Bay of Biscay. Not caught further north.

No similar species.

41

A small, stout, laterally compressed, yellow-brown fish with its scales in oblique rows. Two dorsal fins, the first black and venomously spiny; the second like anal fin. Sharp venomous spine on gill cover. Large oblique mouth. Eyes on top of head.

Found on the seabed from low-tide level to 50m deep, buried in sand, leaving top of head and back exposed; venomous spines can cause very painful wounds to bathers. They feed at night on crustaceans, other fishes, bivalve molluscs and worms.

From Denmark in the North Sea and the Shetland Isles in the Atlantic, south around the British Isles to north Africa and the Mediterranean. Weevers are often caught by shrimp fishermen who have to take care sorting their catch.

Greater Weever is a much longer, grey-brown fish with irregular dark markings. It has similar venomous spines and spines in front of the eyes; its pectoral fins are notched. Buries itself in sand 30–100m deep, from coast of Sweden to Mediterranean.

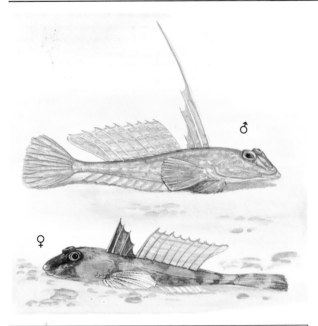

♂

♀

Small fish with a broad head, four spines on each gill cover and spiny fins. Its skin is slimy. Male has bright yellow and blue stripes, and enormously long curved spines on the first dorsal fin. Female has shorter spines and a dull brown body.

Dragonets live on sandy seabeds, around 50m deep. They feed on small crustaceans, bivalves and worms. During spawning the male displays in front of the female; in the display the colourful fins play an important role.

Found from the coast of Norway south in the North Sea, and all around the British Isles to the Mediterranean.

Two other Dragonets found in European seas are smaller and less common. Spotted Dragonet grows 14cm long at most; male and female are brown with blue and dark brown spots instead of stripes. In deeper water, 90–300m, especially over sand.

43

An elongated fish with two separate dorsal fins, first spiny, second with soft rays. Pelvic fins well forward on belly. Anal fin has three spines. Gill cover has teeth on lower edge. Blue or grey back, silvery flanks, white or yellowish belly.

Very common in coastal waters and estuaries in summer, around rocks, over mud and sand. Large fish are mainly solitary, younger ones form schools. A voracious predator on other fishes, squid and crustaceans.

Found around southern coasts of the British Isles, south along the Atlantic coast and throughout the Mediterranean. A popular angling fish.

The chocolate brown Dusky Perch is a related Mediterranean fish; its spiny front dorsal fin and soft hind dorsal fin are continuous. It lives among rocks and in caves at depths of 20–120m. Large fish up to 2m long are now rare due to overfishing.

44

Pagellus bogareveo   up to **50cm**

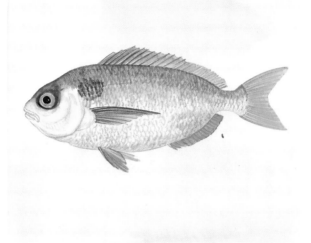

Deep bodied fish with large eyes and one dorsal fin, its front half
spiny. Front teeth curved and sharp, side teeth numerous, small
and rounded. Greyish-red with silver belly and reddish fins;
usually with dark spot at front end of lateral line.

Younger fish are found over rough ground close inshore, older
fish over sandy or muddy seabeds in deeper waters of the
continental shelf, down to 200m. They feed on fishes,
echinoderms, lobsters and crabs.

Common south and west of British Isles, south to the Canaries
and the Mediterranean. In summer they migrate into the North
Sea and reach the coast of Norway. A good-flavoured food fish
and commercially important. Popular with anglers.

The related Black Sea Bream is similar in shape but has grey or
silvery sides, dark grey or black back, and dusky vertical bars
across back and sides. It lives over rocks in the Mediterranean
and north to the south and west coasts of the British Isles.

Large fish with a fleshy fin between dorsal fin and tail. Silvery blue-green back, silver sides and belly; small black round and x-shaped spots above lateral line. Tail peduncle narrow. 10–13 scales between fleshy fin and lateral line.

In the sea, salmon travel widely, feeding on crustaceans and other fishes. Mature salmon migrate into rivers to spawn far upstream in winter. Young salmon swim down to the sea after 1–3 years in the rivers.

Found in the Baltic, North Sea and north Atlantic, south to the Bay of Biscay. A valuable food fish commanding high prices; centre of an important fishing and fish-farming industry. Narrow tail peduncle provides a good hand grip.

River Salmon change colour to greenish or brownish, mottled with orange; jaws of spawning males become hooked. **Trout** have a deep tail peduncle giving no grip for the hands; they have 13–16 scales from the adipose fin to the lateral line.

Salmo trutta trutta

up to **140cm**

A large silvery fish with reddish spots on back, sides and gill covers. It has a fleshy fin between the dorsal and tail fins. Tail peduncle deep, giving no hand grip. 13–16 scales between adipose fin and lateral line.

Mature Sea Trout migrate into rivers to spawn far upstream in winter. Young swim down to the sea where they travel widely, feeding on other fishes and crustaceans. When they mature they return to the rivers to spawn.

Found around the north Atlantic coast, around Iceland, in the Baltic and North Seas, south to the Bay of Biscay. Important food fishes, both commercially and for anglers. They command high prices.

Not all trout migrate to the sea. Landlocked forms (Brown Trout and Lake Trout) are smaller and darker. The related Arctic Charr, with its metallic blue or green back and silver belly, is another food fish from the Arctic and Atlantic Oceans.

COMMON EEL
up to **1m**

Anguilla anguilla

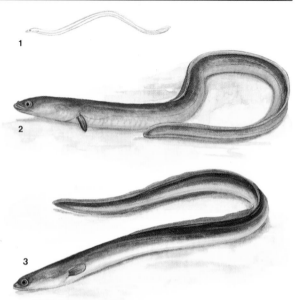

A slimy, cylindrical fish with dorsal, anal and tail fins joined together. Lower jaw longer than upper jaw. Pectoral fins small and rounded, pelvic fins absent. Dorsal fin originates far behind the pectorals. Scales minute and embedded in skin.

Young eels (elvers) live around Atlantic coasts, changing into yellow eels when about 8cm long. Many then enter rivers but others stay in coastal waters. After several years they change into silver eels and migrate to the Sargasso Sea to spawn.

Yellow eels lie in the mud of coastal waters, estuaries and rivers during the day, feeding by night on crustaceans and small fishes. Silver eels do not feed. Both silver eels and yellow eels are important commercial fishes.

Elvers (**1**) are small and transparent. **Yellow Eels** (**2**) are dark on the back and have yellow bellies; males grow up to 40cm, females up to 60cm. **Silver Eels** (**3**) have even darker backs and larger eyes, their sides and bellies are silver.

Like a large Common Eel. But it is scaleless, its upper jaw is longer than its lower, its pectoral fins pointed. Dorsal fin starts close behind pectoral fins. Colour variable, light or dark brown back, belly light gold or white, sides may be grey.

Found in intertidal areas on rocky shores, larger ones in deeper water or deep pools. They hunt crustaceans and other fishes. Adults migrate into deep water (3,000–4,000m) to spawn, between Gibraltar and the Azores, also in the Mediterranean.

Exclusively marine (in contrast to Common Eels). Congers are found to the south and west of British Isles, in the Mediterranean and down the African coast. They are caught on long lines and eaten in France and Spain.

Moray Eel grows up to 130cm long; it is dark brown with yellow spots and has no pectoral fins. Its large sharp teeth can inflict a dangerous, often septic bite. Found in crevices on rocky shores in the Mediterranean but rare in the Atlantic.

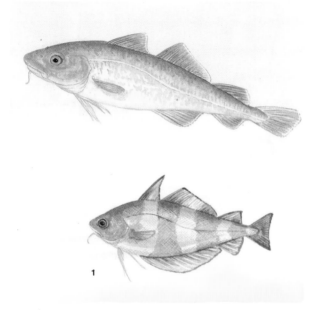

1

A large fish with a long barbel on the chin, three rounded dorsal fins and two anal fins. Pelvic fins are on the throat, in front of the pectorals. Back and sides are mottled brown; belly and lateral line white.

Cod swim in tight shoals by day, looser shoals at night, from the shore line to 600m deep, often 30–80m above the seabed. They migrate long distances in search of food or to spawn. They feed on crustaceans, molluscs, worms and other fishes.

Found across the North Atlantic from Canada to northern Europe, south to the Bay of Biscay. Also found in the North and Baltic Seas. Commercially these are very important fishes, the source of cod liver oil as well as fish and chips.

The related **Bib** (**1**) grows only 40cm long; it is copper-coloured with dark bands over the back and a black spot at the base of the pectoral fin. Common over sandy seabeds in coastal waters of the North Sea, Atlantic and western Mediterranean.

1

This fish has three dorsal fins, the first high and pointed, others rounded. Pelvic fins are on the throat, in front of pectorals. It has a small chin barbel and a black spot between the pectoral and first dorsal fin; lateral line also black.

Found in local populations, mostly close to the seabed, at depths of 10–300m. They feed on worms, echinoderms, molluscs and fishes. The adults spawn during the winter and the young drift in ocean currents, beneath the umbrellas of jellyfish.

Found from the English Channel north to Iceland, in the North Sea and up the western coast of Norway. Not found in the Baltic. Commercially important fishes, sold fresh and smoked.

Poor-cod (**1**) are small haddock-like fishes (growing 22cm long at most). They are very common in offshore waters of the western Baltic, North Sea, Atlantic and western Mediterranean.

Like cod, with three rounded dorsal fins, two anal fins, and pelvic fins on the throat, but with very small chin barbel. Snout long and pointed. Back dark blue to green, sides and belly silvery, with a dark spot at the base of pectoral fin.

Most commonly found in waters 30–100m deep. They feed just off the bottom, on crustaceans, fishes, also worms and molluscs. They spawn throughout their range and the young often shelter beneath the umbrellas of jellyfish.

A very common fish in the North Sea, also in offshore waters along the western coast of Norway, south around the British Isles to the Mediterranean, and across to Iceland. A commercially important species.

Blue Whiting (**1**) is similar in size but has three widely separated dorsal fins; of the two anals, the first has a very long base and it originates in front of the first dorsal. Huge shoals live in the north Atlantic and Mediterranean.

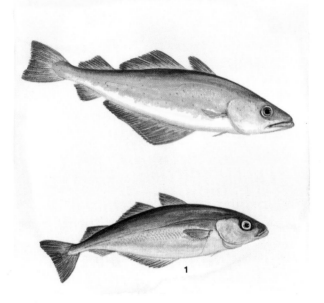

1

Cod-like fish with three dorsal fins and two anal fins, but no barbel. Lateral line dark, arched over pectoral fins. Lower jaw protrudes beyond upper jaw. Back and fins dark in colour, sides yellowish, becoming lighter on belly. Eyes large.

Mainly found in small shoals in inshore waters, to a depth of 200m, usually around rocks or over rough ground. Feeds on fishes and crustaceans.

Common off the southern and western coasts of the British Isles, less common further north to Iceland, in the North Sea and south to Spain. A popular sport fish with inshore anglers.

Saithe (**1**) is caught commercially and sold as coley; similar to Pollack, but has a straight, pale lateral line, smaller eyes and tiny barbel. Lives in small shoals in deeper water than Pollack, from the English Channel north to Norway and Iceland.

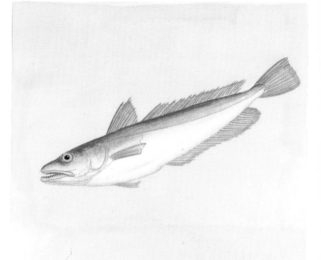

Large elongated fish with two dorsal fins, the first high and pointed, the second long and low; anal fin like second dorsal fin. Mouth large with large hinged teeth; inside of the mouth is dark. Back grey or blue, sides and belly lighter.

Hake feed in mid-water at night, returning to the seabed by day. They mainly eat other fishes. Main spawning grounds lie to the southwest and west of the British Isles; young drift in the currents to inshore waters.

Found in the north Atlantic from northern Norway to Iceland, south in the North Sea and west of the British Isles to the Mediterranean, in water 150–550m deep in winter, in shallower waters in summer. An important commercial fish.

The related Torsk has one long narrow dorsal fin and a long narrow anal fin, both joined to the tail and all edged in white. It swims in small shoals in deep water, from Norway to Iceland and off the western coast of Scotland and Ireland.

54

Molva molva

1

Large elongated fish with a long barbel and two dorsal fins, the first rounded, second long and narrow like the anal. Pectoral fins short. Eyes small. Marbled bronze-green, lighter on the sides and belly; with a dark spot on the first dorsal fin.

A deep-water fish, found near the seabed around rocks, in water up to 400m deep, older fish in deeper waters. They are predators, feeding mainly on other fishes.

Found in the north Atlantic from Iceland to northern Norway, south in the North Sea and west of the British Isles to the Bay of Biscay. A valuable commercial fish, mainly salted and dried and eaten in southern Europe.

Spanish Ling (**1**) is similar in shape but blue-silver in colour, with a grey back, large eyes and long pelvic fins that reach back past the pectorals. It lives in deep water from the southwest coast of Britain to the Mediterranean.

Dark green-grey fish with silver sides, striped from head to tail by grey bands. Belly and pectoral fins white. Mouth small with a thick, warty upper lip. Both dorsal fins and anal fin are short-based; first dorsal fin has four spines.

Mullet swim in formation in close shoals, in coastal waters and estuaries. May leap from the water if disturbed. Feed in spring and summer, mostly on tiny planktonic organisms. Appear to hibernate in deeper offshore waters and not feed in winter.

All along the coasts of northern Europe and the British Isles, in the Mediterranean and Black Sea. Numbers increase in far northern waters in spring and summer. A popular angling fish but difficult to catch.

Thin-lipped Grey Mullet is less common. Similar to above species but with a very thin upper lip and no warts. Found in shallow coastal waters and estuaries from south and west of British Isles southwards.

A small, silvery, eel-like fish, tinged with yellow on back and sides. It has a protruding lower jaw and an upper jaw which can be moved forward to form a long tube. One very long dorsal fin (with soft rays) and a long anal fin. Pelvic fins absent.

Very common from the midshore level of sandy beaches to sandy seabeds 30m deep. The fish may swim in shoals or lie half-buried in the sand. Can be dug for bait on sandy beaches. They feed on smaller fishes and worms.

Coasts of Scandinavia and Iceland, into the Baltic and south to Portugal; rare in the Mediterranean. A vital food fish for many commercially important species, like herring, cod, mackerel etc. Anglers use them for bait.

One of five sand eels in European seas, three others in deep water. Greater Sand Eel lives in inshore waters (with a similar distribution to the Sand Eel illustrated); it grows up to 30cm long and has a black spot on each side of the snout.

57

Herring-like fish, with a deep, rather flattened body and a line of keeled scales on its belly. Upper jaw notched in the midline. Brilliant blue back, silver sides and belly; sides of head and flanks golden, with six or seven dark spots on flanks.

Sexually mature fishes are found in estuaries and river mouths in summer. They go there to spawn (and their numbers are much reduced by pollution because of this). Young move down into the sea in autumn. They feed on smaller fishes and crustaceans.

Frequent on southwestern coasts of Europe and in the Mediterranean, much less common in the North Sea.

Allis Shad is larger (up to 60cm long) and usually has only one spot on the flank. It is much rarer in northern European waters, becoming more common south of Ireland. Adults swim far up into rivers to spawn.

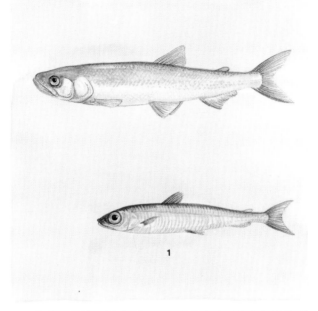

1

A slender fish with an extra fleshy fin on the back near the tail. Dorsal fin placed well back. Tail distinctly forked. Mouth large with needle-like teeth. It has a light olive green back, a silver stripe along each side, creamy white belly.

Rarely found far from the shore. Adults migrate into river mouths in winter, spawn there in spring, then return to the sea. The young live in estuaries. Smelt are active predators, feeding on a wide variety of other fishes and crustaceans.

Found in the Baltic, North Sea and Atlantic, south to the Bay of Biscay. They are of little commercial value, although caught for fish oil and cattle feed. Fresh smelts smell of cucumber.

The similar **Argentine** (**1**) is a more slender fish; its dorsal fin is directly in front of the pelvic fin. It lives in water from 50–200m deep, over mud and sandy seabeds from the north Atlantic to the Mediterranean.

1

A slender, silvery fish with a dark blue back. Large, round thin scales. One dorsal fin, one anal fin. Pectoral fins are quite low on the body, pelvic fins on the belly. The mouth points upwards. All fins are soft, without spines.

Found in extremely large shoals in offshore waters from the surface down to 200m. Shoals migrate in regular seasonal routes, following their food, mainly planktonic crustaceans. They also migrate to and from the spawning grounds each year.

Found in Arctic and Atlantic Oceans from North America to Europe, as far south as France. Also in North and Baltic Seas. Commercially important fishes in danger of overfishing: strict quotas are now applied. Young are caught as whitebait.

Sprat (1) is smaller, up to 14cm long; it has a line of spiny scales along the length of the belly from the throat to the anus. It lives in large shoals in the inshore waters from northern Scandinavia to the Mediterranean. Commercially important.

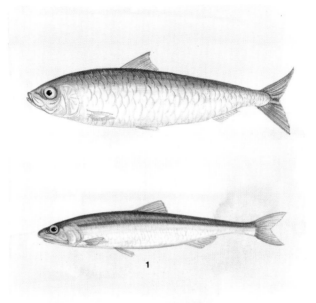

1

Like a small herring but with a more rounded body. Gill cover has pronounced radial ridges. Dorsal fin originates in front of the pelvic fins. Back greenish, sides golden, shading to silver-white beneath. No spiny scales on belly.

Found in large moving shoals, swimming at 25–55m by night. They feed on planktonic crustaceans and fish eggs. Spawning shoals produce millions of eggs.

Common from the English Channel south to the Mediterranean, migrating northwards into the North Sea in some years, especially in a hot summer. Commercially important fishes; most young fish are canned.

Anchovy (**1**) is distinctively coloured, with a green back clearly demarcated from the silver sides and belly. It is found in huge shoals from the North Sea to the Mediterranean. It is commercially important; usually eaten salted and canned.

SCAD OR HORSE MACKEREL
up to **40cm**
Trachurus trachurus

Heavy-headed fish with two spines on belly, large bony scales along the lateral line. Two dorsal fins, the first with high spines, the second long, sloping and similar to anal. Greenish-grey back, sides and belly silver, black spot on gill cover.

Found in large pelagic shoals in inshore waters to 55m deep, in shallower water in summer, often over a sandy bottom. They feed on a variety of pelagic fishes, also on crustaceans and squid. Young fish often found under the umbrellas of jellyfish.

From the northern Atlantic and North Sea south to the coast of Africa, Mediterranean and Black Sea. Not commercially important in northern Europe but caught further south. Eaten like sardines, fresh or smoked.

The related **Pilot-fish** swim with sharks, turtles, even ships; they are found in the Mediterranean and southern Atlantic, more rarely north to the English Channel. **Mackerel** are similar in appearance but are not related to Scad.

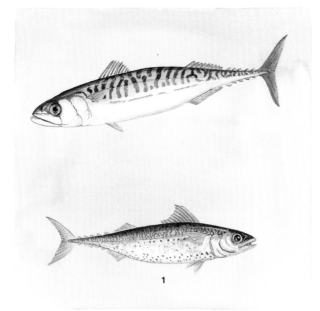

1

Mackerel have an iridescent blue-green back crossed with dark, curved stripes, silver sides and belly. The two dorsal fins are widely separated. Small finlets follow behind both the second dorsal and the anal fins.

Mackerel swim in enormous shoals in the upper waters of the open sea in spring and summer, feeding on pelagic crustaceans and other fishes. They retire to deeper waters in winter, stay on the seabed and almost hibernate, not feeding.

Found in the north Atlantic from the Baltic to Iceland, in the North Sea and south to the Mediterranean. An important commercial fish, eaten fresh and smoked. They must be eaten soon after catching as the flesh deteriorates very quickly.

The related **Spanish Mackerel** (**1**) has black spots on its silver-yellow sides and belly. It is found from the Bay of Biscay to the Mediterranean and Black Sea, where it is caught commercially. **Horse Mackerel** is unrelated to these two fishes.

TUNNY OR BLUE-FIN TUNA
up to **245cm**; **300kg**   *Tunnus thynnus*

A very large fish with two dorsal fins almost touching; both very concave in outline. There are several small finlets behind the anal and second dorsal fins. Pectoral fins short. Back dark blue, sides white with silvery spots, belly white.

Common in offshore waters and in the open ocean, in schools of same size fishes, larger tunny swimming with dolphins. They feed on other fishes, herring, mackerel, sand eels etc, also on squid. They may leap out of the water in a feeding frenzy.

Found all year in southern Atlantic and in Mediterranean, migrating north to the North Sea and north Atlantic in spring and summer. Caught in nets or on long lines. However if tunny are caught with nets, any dolphins with them die too.

Long-fin Tunny has long pectoral fins which reach back as far as the second dorsal fin. It is brown with an iridescent blue band along each side. Common from Bay of Biscay to the Mediterranean. Another important commercial fish.

A very large fish with a distinctive long sword on the snout. Sword flattened and oval in cross-section. Tail half-moon shaped. Single dorsal fin high and near the head. Pelvic fins absent. There is a keel on each side of the tail.

Solitary fishes; they can be spotted in the open sea by the high dorsal fin breaking the surface of the water. They go on long migrations. They feed on shoals of other fishes, herring, mackerel, cod etc., also squid.

Not common in northern waters. More common in Mediterranean and off the Portuguese coast. Commercially important in southern European seas. Mostly eaten fresh. Also a popular angling fish.

No similar species.

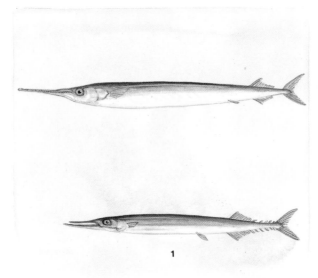

A very long fish with beak-like jaws and sharp teeth. It has a green or dark blue back, silver flanks and yellowish belly. Anal and pelvic fins are yellow with darker edges, the other fins are dark. Anal and dorsal fins are similar.

Lives in large migratory shoals, often with **Mackerel**, in the upper layers of the open sea and in coastal waters. The shoals migrate widely, following the planktonic animals on which they feed.

Found in the Atlantic, North Sea, Baltic and Mediterranean (more commonly in summer in inshore waters). Of little commercial value but often caught with mackerel; they may leap out of the water to avoid the nets. A good angling fish.

Skipper (1) is smaller related fish (up to 45cm long). Its dorsal and anal fins are followed by several small fins. Found in shoals in the Atlantic and Mediterranean, migrating north as far as the Baltic in summer. They may 'skip' out of the water.

Pipefishes

Very elongated fishes, up to 45cm long; body covered with bony plates, giving them an angular appearance. Snout long & tubular with very small mouth at the end. Feeble swimmers, mostly propelling themselves along with their dorsal fins. Males carry eggs until they hatch, stuck to the belly or in a pouch, depending on species. Six European species, mostly found in shallow water among seaweeds or in eelgrass beds. Med., Atlantic, N. Sea, Baltic. **Great Pipefish** (1) is one of the largest & most familiar.

Seahorse (2)

Distinctive small fishes, covered with angular plates. Found in shallow inshore waters, among seaweeds or in eelgrass beds. They propel themselves along with their dorsal fins or hold onto seaweeds with their tails. They have protruding eyes which can move independently to spot prey, small crustaceans which are sucked into the tiny mouth. Males carry eggs in a brood pouch until they hatch. Found from English Channel south to Med. & Black Sea; more common from Bay of Biscay south.

67

OTHER FISHES

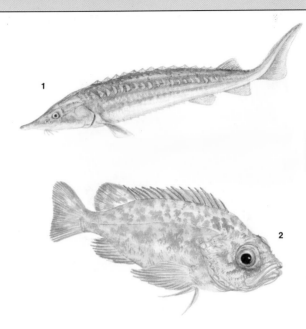

Sturgeon (1)
has five rows of bony plates
running along length of body.
Snout long with two pairs of
barbels. Blue-black back,
lighter sides, white beneath.
Dorsal plates light-coloured,
especially in young fish. Once
quite common, now quite rare
due to overfishing (eggs are
prized as caviar). Adults live in
sea at about 20–50m deep, but
swim into rivers to spawn; only
populations left are centred on
the R. Gironde in France & Bay
of Biscay; R. Guadalquivir in
Spain & Gulf of Cadiz; L.
Ladoga in Russia & Gulf of
Finland.

Redfish (2)
A large, bright red fish, more
than 1m long. Its single dorsal
fin has two parts; the first with
15 strong spines, the second
part with soft rays. Head large
& heavy with spines on gill
covers. A deep-water fish, found
in north Atlantic and N. Sea.
Economically important, mostly
sold frozen, on the continent &
in N. America. Also known as
Norway Haddock.

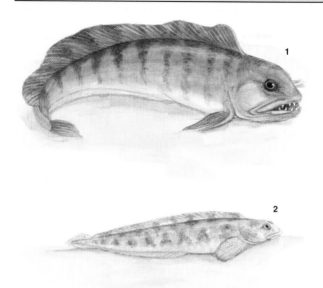

Wolf-fish (1)

Quite a large fish, up to 1.2m long, with large dog-like teeth in the front of the jaws, flattened grinding teeth in sides. Dorsal fin long & narrow. Scales far apart & deeply embedded. No pelvic fins. A bottom-living fish, older ones living in deep water to 300m deep, younger ones in shallower water, sometimes at low-tide level in summer. N. Sea & along coast of Norway, round Scotland to Iceland & N. America. Sold as rock salmon or rockfish in Britain.

Eel-pout (2)

A slimy, eel-like fish, around 30cm long when mature. It has a large head & tapering body. Long flexible dorsal & anal fins are continuous with tail fin. Pelvic fins long & slender. Pectoral fins large & rounded. Scales minute & embedded in the skin. Lies on the bottom in water 4–10m deep; often buried in mud or beneath stones. N. Sea along the eastern coast of Britain to the west coast of Norway; very common from Scotland northwards, where it also lives on the shore. Eaten fresh, salted or smoked.

OTHER FISHES

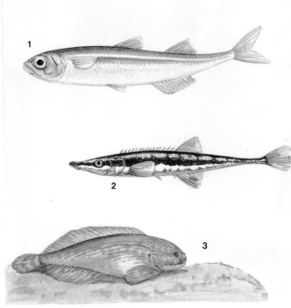

Sand-smelt (1)
A small fish, up to 15cm long with a bright silver line along each side. Swims in dense shoals near the surface; in brackish water, river mouths, estuaries, around docks & saltings, sometimes in large rock pools. West & south coast of British Isles, south to the Med. More common in summer in the northern parts of its range.

Sea Stickleback (2)
A small, very elongated fish, 10–15cm long. It has 14–15 spines on its back. Found in estuaries & among seaweeds on shore. Around British Isles,

coast of Norway & Baltic Sea. Male makes a nest among seaweeds, entices female to lay her eggs there, then guards eggs & young.

Sea Snail (3)
A soft, slimy tadpole-like fish, up to 18cm long. Its pelvic fins form a suction disc; dorsal & anal fins are very long & attached to tail fin. Lives in shallow water & estuaries of Irish Sea & west coast of Scotland, N. Sea & coast of Norway. Montagu's Sea-snail is a smaller species found on the shore.

1

Slimy-skinned, eel-like animal, with no jaws but a horny sucking disc around the mouth. Large eyes. Seven gill openings behind the head. Two separate dorsal fins. No paired fins. Colour brown, mottled with black, becoming pale grey beneath.

Adult lampreys feed parasitically on a wide range of fishes (including salmon, cod, haddock, sharks etc.), attaching themselves with the sucking disc, rasping at the skin and then sucking the blood. They kill smaller fish, weaken larger ones.

Found locally in the North Sea, Atlantic and Mediterranean. Adult lampreys live in the sea but swim into rivers in summer, to breed. The young spend up to five years in fresh water as larvae, then metamorphose and descend to the sea as adults.

Young adult River Lampreys live in coastal waters; they are golden-brown and smaller. **Hagfish** (1) has no fins and barbels around its lipless mouth. Found in Atlantic and North Sea, they attack fish on long lines, dead fish and crustaceans.

Star-shaped echinoderms with a central disc and five or more arms (no clear division between disc and arms), and a double row of tube feet in an open groove beneath each arm. Tube feet end in suckers. Mouth on underside of disc, anus on upper side.

Starfishes move slowly about on their tube feet. All are carnivorous, many feeding on molluscs. Common Starfishes will pull bivalves open with their tube feet; other starfish swallow their prey whole.

Many species occur in Atlantic, North Sea and Mediterranean. Found under rocks or in pools of lower shore and into deep water. Some are flattened, living on or burrowing into sandy seabeds; cushion stars are more rounded and live on rocks.

Some starfish are tough but pliable, like **Common Starfish** (1); this is a pest on mussel beds. Others are hard with close-set plates, like the **Cushion Starlet** (2); this very small starfish clings to rocks on the lower shore, as do **Sunstars** (3).

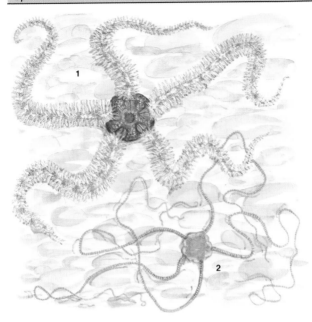

Star-shaped echinoderms. Central disc is small and sharply divided from the spiny arms. Body covered by hard plates. Beneath each arm, the groove containing tube feet is covered; tube feet lack suckers. Mouth is on underside of disc. No anus.

Brittlestars move jerkily, using their whole arms. Tube feet are used for feeding, not for walking. Some feed on planktonic animals, capturing them with mucous strands; others shovel mud into their mouths and digest the food within.

Found from midshore to deep water in Mediterranean, Atlantic and North Sea, in some places in huge numbers, where water currents bring the plankton they feed on. On shore some burrow in sand, others hide in pools, beneath rocks or seaweed.

Common Brittlestars (**1**) live under rocks and seaweed from lower shore to deeper water. **Long-armed Brittlestars** (**2**) burrow into the sand; they are found from midshore to deeper water.

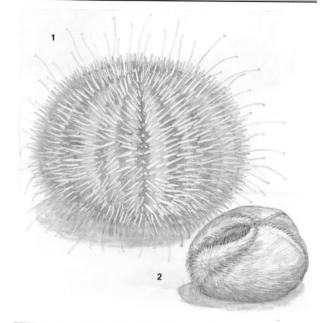

Globular or heart-shaped echinoderms. The brittle case is made of interlocking plates; it bears many long spines, each on a small tubercle, and has five double rows of holes through which tube feet project in life. Mouth at the bottom, anus on top.

Urchins are often gregarious. Regular urchins (round ones) live around rocks, among seaweeds, in pools of rocky shores. Heart urchins burrow into sand or mud. Fragments of their cases are often washed ashore.

They live on the lower shore and in coastal waters to 100m deep. Many species live in the Mediterranean, others in the Atlantic north to the English Channel, a few in the North Sea and Baltic. Their cases are often sold as souvenirs.

Common Sea Urchin (**1**) is edible. It is common just below low-tide level in Atlantic and North Sea. **Sea Potato** or Heart Urchin (**2**) burrows into sand below low-tide level, using its spines; found in Mediterranean, Atlantic and North Sea.

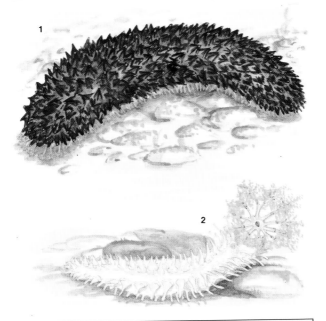

Leathery but limp echinoderms resembling gherkins. The mouth is at one end, surrounded by a circle of retractable tentacles. Anus is at other end. Some species have three or five rows of tube feet (with suckers). Others lack tube feet.

Some live in rock crevices, others move slowly over the seabed or burrow into sand. They collect food with their tentacles. Some species eject white sticky threads if threatened (hence cotton spinner), entangling or distracting their predators.

Several species are found in the Atlantic, North Sea and Mediterranean. Small species live on the shore, larger ones in deeper waters. Some Mediterranean species are edible.

Cotton Spinner (**1**) is usually about 12cm long; it has three rows of tube feet on the under side. **Sea Gherkin** (**2**) has five rows of tube feet. Both live among subtidal rocks, around southern and western coasts of British Isles and France.

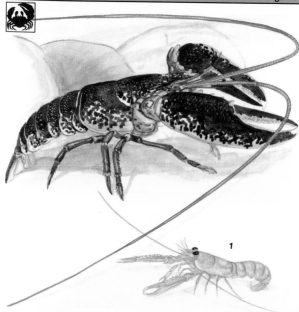

1

Large, heavily armoured, blue-black crustacean with a heavy carapace over head and thorax, and massive, unequal pincers. Long abdomen ends in a tail fin which can be tucked under body. Antennae longer than body. Eyes on stalks.

A scavenger, walking over seabed at night, searching for worms, bivalves, dead fish etc. If in danger it can swim suddenly backwards and uses its claws for defence as well as for handling food. Females carry eggs on the swimmerets in summer.

Found in offshore waters, from lowtide level to 40m deep, among rocks and seaweeds, hiding in crevices by day with only claws and antennae showing. Northern Atlantic and North Sea to Mediterranean. Caught commercially in lobster pots.

Dublin Bay Prawns (**1**) are similar but much smaller (up to 20cm long), with long narrow claws. They hide by day in soft muddy or sandy seabeds, in offshore waters 40–200m deep, in the Atlantic and Mediterranean. They are caught and sold as scampi.

76

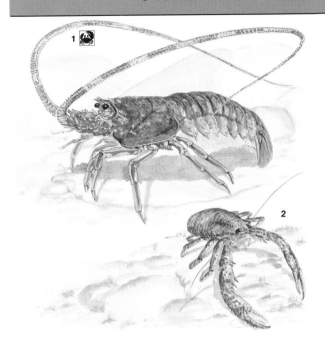

Crawfish or **Spiny Lobster** (**1**)
grows up to 50cm long, has a
heavily armoured, spiny body
but only has small pincers, not
large claws. The spines can
inflict nasty cuts. They are
caught in lobster pots, especially
in the Med., & eaten as
langouste on the continent. Also
found in the Gulf Stream on the
Atlantic coasts of Portugal,
France & the British Isles. They
live among rocks, usually
offshore.

Squat Lobsters (**2**)
A group of small lobsters
(growing up to 12cm long at
most, usually much smaller),
with a squat appearance which
comes from the way the
abdomen is turned under the
thorax. They have large claws
on the first pair of walking legs
(& can be aggressive); the fifth
pair of walking legs is reduced.
Several species occur in the N.
Sea, Atlantic & Med. They live
in crevices & under stones on
the lower shore & in offshore
waters.

77

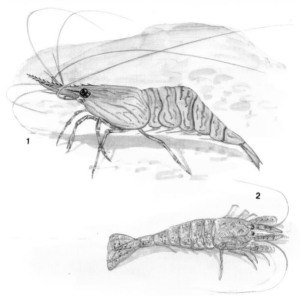

Relatively small, swimming crustaceans; head and thorax covered by carapace. Thorax bears five pairs of 'walking' legs; first two pairs of legs possess small pincers. Abdomen bears five pairs of swimmerets and ends in a tail fan. Eyes on stalks.

Scavengers, searching for food by walking slowly, sweeping the seabed with their antennae. They may swim gently about or dart backwards if danger threatens. Females carry eggs on the swimmerets in summer (they are said to be 'in berry').

Many species are found in the Baltic, North Sea, Atlantic and Mediterranean; in rock pools, at the edge of the sea, among seaweeds, on sandy beaches, estuaries and salt marshes, and in offshore waters. Many are edible and caught commercially.

Prawns, like the **Common Prawn** (**1**) have antennae that are at least as long as the body and a long rostrum between the eyes. Shrimps, like the **Common Shrimp** (**2**) have no rostrum; and their antennae are shorter than their body.

A crab that lives in an empty snail shell. Abdomen coiled and soft, protected by the shell. Head and three pairs of walking legs project out of the shell; the first pair of legs bears large, but unequal claws. Eyes on stalks. Antennae long.

A scavenger. If danger threatens the crab withdraws into the shell, blocking the opening with its large right claw. It is difficult to extract since it clings to the shell with its back legs. An important food source for sea birds.

Found on shores and in subtidal waters, often on sandy beaches and sand flats but also in rock pools and beneath seaweeds. North Sea, Atlantic and Mediterranean. Shell often covered by barnacles, hydroids or sponges, and may carry anemones.

Several hermit crabs live in European waters, all similar but with differing distributions. Small ones live in topshells, winkle shells etc., larger ones in whelk shells.

79

1

A large crab, with a broad, heavy, rounded carapace covering head and thorax; carapace has scalloped edges like a piecrust. Abdomen small and tucked under body. This crab has a pair of large claws and four pairs of walking legs. Eyes are on stalks.

Edible Crabs hide on rough, rocky seabeds beneath kelp, under rocks or in crevices, coming out to dig for bivalve molluscs or to scavenge for edible tidbits. Watch out for its claws!

Found from north Atlantic and North Sea to Mediterranean. Smaller crabs live in pools on the lower shore, large crabs in water 30m deep in summer; they all migrate into deeper water in winter. Caught commercially in lobster pots.

Masked Crab (1) is only 4cm across. The furrows on the carapace resemble a mask. It lives buried in clean sand on lower shores and in subtidal waters, leaving only its long hairy antennae and claws exposed. Found in Atlantic and Med.

A medium-sized crab; the carapace has rounded, saw-like teeth on the front margin. Eyes on stalks. Abdomen tucked beneath the body. The last joint of the back legs is somewhat flattened with a sharp, pointed tip. Aggressive, with large claws.

Shore Crabs bury themselves in sand, hide under stones or in crevices, under seaweeds. They are scavengers, feeding on dead fish, snails etc. Eaten by fishes and seabirds. They spread their claws threateningly if disturbed.

Abundant on all kinds of seashores and in estuaries, from mid to low tide level. Coasts from Baltic and North Sea to Atlantic and Mediterranean. Eaten on the continent. Empty shells and claws are often found on the shore.

Velvet Crab (**1**) is a hairy crab with blue lines on its legs. Last joint of back legs is flat and rounded, like a paddle. Found under stones or seaweeds of lower shore and subtidal waters, in Atlantic and Mediterranean. Aggressive.

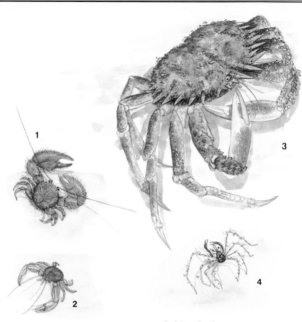

Porcelain Crabs
Small crabs that appear to have only three pairs of legs (the last pair is very small). **Hairy Porcelain Crab** (1) is 4cm across at most; has broad flattened claws almost as large as flattened body; its legs & the edges of its body are hairy. It lives on shore, under stones on muddy sand & gravel. **Minute Porcelain Crab** (2) has a round shiny body only 1cm across, & long, slender, unequal claws. It lives under stones & among kelp holdfasts on lower shore & in offshore waters. Both occur in the N. Sea, Atlantic & Med.

Spider Crabs
have triangular bodies, long legs & relatively small claws. They camouflage themselves by attaching pieces of seaweed, sponges etc. to the carapace. Several species occur in the N. Sea, Atlantic & Med., more in the south. **Spiny Spider Crabs** (3) are caught in lobster pots from the English Channel to the Med.; they grow up to 20cm across. **Long-legged Spider Crab** (4) is widespread on European coasts & the most common on the shore, living under stones & kelp. Like most spider crabs, it is small, only about 1cm across.

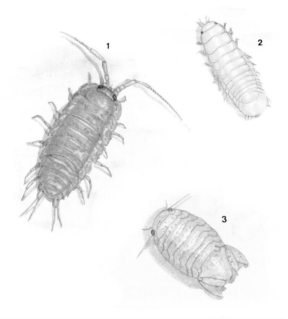

Small flattened crustaceans, like marine woodlice, with a body of
many similar segments. Seven pairs of legs on thorax.
Abdominal legs flattened and close to the body. Two pairs of
antennae, outer ones large; inner ones small. Eyes large.

Most isopods feed on decaying fragments of seaweeds and dead
animals. Females carry the developing young in a brood pouch
under the body. On the shore, they hide in damp places while
the tide is out.

Many species are found on the shores and in the offshore waters
of the Baltic and North Seas, Atlantic and Mediterranean, on
sandy beaches, rocky coasts, estuaries and salt-marshes, in
crevices, among kelps or under stones.

Sea-slaters (1) hide in rock crevices of the splash zone by day,
emerging at night. They grow up to 4cm long. **The Gribble** (2)
bores into timber on the lower shore. ***Sphaeroma rugicauda*** (3)
lives in estuaries and pools in salt marshes.

83

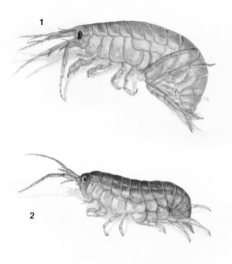

Small, laterally compressed, often curved crustaceans, with large eyes and two pairs of antennae. The body has many similar segments with five pairs of legs on the thorax. Abdomen has three pairs of legs (swimmerets) and ends in a tail fan.

Two main groups of sandhoppers. **Gammarus** species (**1**) and their relatives lie on their sides and the tail fan is used to push the animal around. **Talitrus saltator** (**2**) and its relatives walk around upright, and use their tail fan to help them jump.

Many species of sandhoppers are found on the shore, from the Baltic and North Sea, to the Atlantic and Mediterranean. Some live in sand (hence sand-hoppers) or shingle, more live under stones or decaying seaweed on the strand line.

Gammarus species (**1**) are abundant everywhere, under stones, on mud and the lower shore, many in estuaries. **Talitrus saltator** (**2**) lives among rotting seaweeds on the strandline of sandy shores.

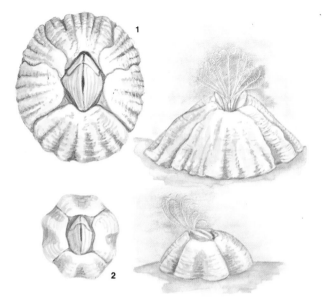

Volcano-shaped crustaceans, with four or six limy plates covering the body. The opening at the top can be closed by four smaller plates. It opens in water to reveal six feathery legs, which are thrust out over and over again.

When barnacles thrust their legs out they are feeding, catching small pieces of food. Their larvae are released into the sea in spring; the larvae swim in the sea for some time, then settle head first on the rocks and change into adult barnacles.

Barnacles cover the rocks on the middle levels of the shore, especially on exposed coasts, making the rocks look grey. They are still present but less abundant in sheltered bays. Found from Baltic and North Sea to Atlantic and Mediterranean.

Common Acorn Barnacle (**1**) is abundant on Atlantic coasts. It has six plates and a diamond-shaped opening. Similar species vary in the form of the opening. **Australian Barnacle** (**2**) is common on sheltered rocks. It has only four plates.

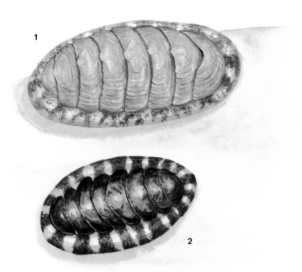

Flattened, oval molluscs with eight articulating plates on the back, their edges buried in a fleshy girdle. The body has a head at the front, anus at the back, muscular foot beneath. Gills lie along each side, in a groove between girdle and foot.

Chitons cling tightly to rocks, moving about very slowly and grazing on algae with a rasping tongue. Then returning to the same place on the rock. They curl up like woodlice if prised loose.

Many species live on rocky shores and in offshore waters, from the north Atlantic, southern Baltic and North Sea to the Mediterranean. They are often inconspicuous, hiding in rock crevices or under stones.

Lepidochiton cinereus (**1**) lives on many shores. Its girdle has large spines; it varies in colour from dull red to grey-brown or green. *Tonicella rubra* (**2**) lives on lower shores and in offshore waters; it has a granular girdle and shiny plates.

1

A snail with a conical, thick, ribbed shell, its apex just off centre, varying in colour from greyish to brown. Beneath the shell can be seen a strong muscular foot, with head and tentacles at the front. Mouth has a rasping tongue inside.

Limpets cling tightly to the rocks when the tide is out, returning to the same depression each time; they are difficult to dislodge. When the tide is in, they move about and feed, grazing on new growths on seaweeds and rocks.

Found on rocky shores in the mid and upper tidal levels. North Sea and Atlantic coasts of Europe, south to the English Channel. A similar species is found in the Mediterranean.

This is one of several European limpets. **Keyhole Limpet** (**1**) has a hole at the apex of the shell. It grows up to 4cm long. It lives on rocks from the lower shore to 20m deep, in North Sea and Atlantic. A similar species lives in the Mediterranean.

Snails with strong, (usually) conical shells, coiled with only a few whorls. Aperture is rounded and is sealed with a horny operculum when the animal is alive. The body has a strong foot and the head has tentacles.

Their tough shells protect these molluscs from the heaviest seas. They can survive on the most exposed shores: the shells can be rolled by the waves without damage. They do not cling to rocks.

Common on rocky shores and in estuaries from the splash zone downwards, in crevices, among seaweeds, in pools. In the Baltic, North Sea, Atlantic and Mediterranean. Edible Winkles are the largest and commercially important.

Edible Winkle (**1**), **Rough Periwinkle** (**2**), **Small Periwinkle** (**3**) and **Flat Periwinkle** (**4**) all live on rocky shores. Small Periwinkles wedge themselves into crevices in the splash zone. Flat Periwinkles may be bright yellow, brown or black.

Snails with strong, broad-based, coiled, top-shaped or rounded shells. When they are worn the underlying mother-of-pearl shows through. The aperture is round, closed by an operculum while the animal is alive.

In rock pools or when the tide is in the animals emerge from their shells, revealing the two tentacles on the head and tentacles on the sides of the foot. They feed by grazing on seaweeds and rocks, like limpets.

Found on rocky shores from midtide level to subtidal waters 150m deep. Several species of topshells live in the Atlantic, North Sea and Mediterranean, each with a different distribution and confined to a different zone on the shore.

Common Topshell (**1**) is the largest, with a shell like a top; found from lower shore to 100m deep in North Sea, Atlantic and Mediterranean. **Grey Topshell** (**2**) lives in pools and under seaweeds on mid and lower shores of Atlantic and North Sea.

89

COMMON WHELK
up to **12cm** tall
Buccinum undatum

Shell is thick and ribbed, with a pointed spire. Aperture oval, ending in short siphonal canal and closed by a horny operculum. Snail has a large foot and a head with tentacles; its siphon is held upright, projecting out through the siphonal canal.

Carnivorous scavenger. Whelks plough through sand and mud, using the upright siphon to draw in a current of water to breathe, and to scent dead animals. Their eggs are laid in spongy egg cases. Empty **egg cases** (**1**) are often washed ashore.

Found in sand and muddy gravel, on lower shores and in offshore waters to 1200m deep. West Baltic, North Sea and Atlantic. Edible. You can 'hear the sea' in an empty shell: they are often washed ashore and hermit crabs use them as homes.

Dog Whelk (**2**) is smaller (up to 2.5cm tall). It lives on Atlantic and North Sea shores among barnacles or mussels, on which it feeds. It bores a hole into the animal with its saw-like tongue. Other whelks live in the Mediterranean.

OTHER GASTROPODS

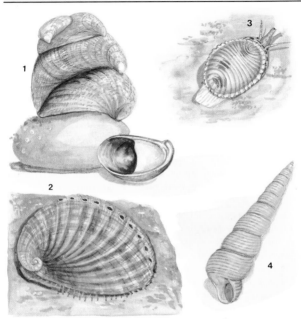

Slipper Limpet (1)
Has a shell like a boat with a low coiled apex & a white platform inside. Lives in chains in shallow inshore waters of Atlantic & N. Sea. Introduced from N. America & now a pest in oyster beds. Shells are often washed ashore.

Ormer (2)
Its ear-shaped, flattened shell has a row of holes along one edge; it grows up to 10cm long. Lives under stones & among rocks on lower shore & in offshore waters. Med. & along Atlantic coast north to Channel Islands.

European Cowrie (3)
Much smaller than tropical cowries, only 12mm long, but with same glossy shell. Living animal has fleshy covering over much of shell. Lives on rocky shores & in offshore waters. Atlantic & Med.

Tower Shell (4)
Narrow tapering shell, up to 6cm tall, with spiral ridges. Lives in large communities in mud or sand in offshore waters; empty shells often washed ashore. North Sea, Atlantic & Med. One of many similar unrelated snails found on European coasts.

SEA-SLUGS
up to **20cm**

Nudibranchia

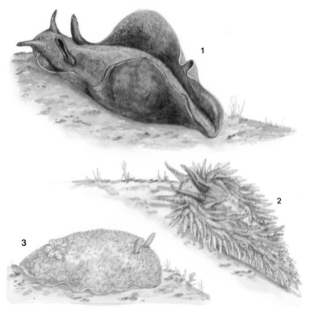

Like land slugs, a group of snails without an external shell. They are more or less flattened and lose their form out of water. They are often striking animals, brightly coloured, with gills on the back. The head has four tentacles.

Sea-slugs can be found crawling among kelps or rocks encrusted with other animals. Some of them can swim. Some feed by grazing on seaweeds; others are carnivorous, grazing on sea-mats, anemones and sponges.

Many species of sea-slugs live in the North Sea, Atlantic and Mediterranean. Most are found in offshore waters as they cannot survive out of water; many come to the shore in summer, to spawn in rock pools or below rocks, and then die.

Sea-hare (**1**) lives among kelps; it can eject purple slime if disturbed. **Common Grey Sea-slug** (**2**) lives under stones and rocks on shore. **Sea Lemon** (**3**) lives in rock pools or in rocky offshore waters. All three occur in the North Sea and Atlantic.

A bivalve mollusc with a smooth, curved, blue-black shell, pointed at one end. Both valves are similar and often encrusted with barnacles. The frilled edge of the mantle shows at the edges when the shell is open.

Found attached to rocks, stones, piers in dense colonies. They are attached by tough threads (the byssus). Filter feeders, extracting tiny food particles from the stream of water drawn into the shell.

Very common from midtide level to about 10m deep. On sandy, rocky and muddy shores, in estuaries. From the Baltic, North Sea and Atlantic to the Mediterranean. Edible. Collected in the wild from unpolluted waters. Also farmed in mussel beds.

Similar Mediterranean Mussel occurs south of British Isles. **Horse Mussel** (1) lives in rock pools and kelp beds from lower shore to about 150m deep; North Sea and Atlantic, south to the Bay of Biscay. It grows abut 8–14cm long and is also edible.

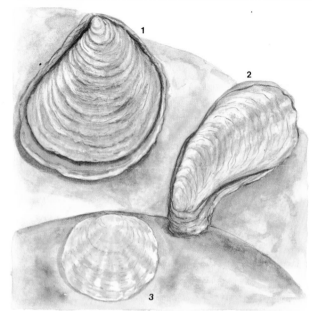

Oysters have thick, irregularly oval or rounded shells, layered in appearance, with irregular, wavy growth lines. Lower valve is flattish and cupped into deeper upper one. Opened, the shells contain the body, surrounded by four dark gills.

Oysters live in dense oyster beds (natural or farmed) on mud or silt, usually in estuaries and inlets. They cement themselves to rocks, stones, seaweeds etc. by the left valve.

The **Common Oyster** (**1**) is found in the North Sea, Atlantic and Mediterranean. **Portuguese Oyster** (**2**) is found around Spain, in the Bay of Biscay; and in commercial beds around the British Isles. Both are edible and commercially important.

The unrelated **Saddle Oyster** (**3**) is found on lower shores and in shallow waters of the Mediterranean and Atlantic; it has a deep rounded cleft at the front of the lower valve. Empty shells are often washed ashore. It grows up to 5cm across.

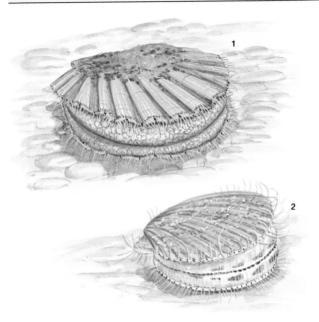

Scallops are distinctive bivalves; their rounded, ribbed shells have 'ears', one on each side of the hinge. The hinge has no teeth. The edge of the mantle is visible when the shells are open; the edge bears many tentacles and eyes.

Unusually for bivalves, scallops can swim, flapping their two valves and moving by a series of convulsive jerks. They swim to avoid predators but also migrate over long distances.

Found on sand and sandy or gravelly mud, in offshore waters of the North Sea, Atlantic and Mediterranean, from the lowest tide level downwards. They do not burrow but lie on the bottom. Both species illustrated are edible and commercially important.

Several scallops occur in European seas. **Great Scallop** (**1**) has one flat valve, one convex valve, and symmetrical ears. It is the largest European scallop. **Queen Scallop** (**2**) has two convex valves and asymmetrical ears. It grows up to 9m across.

A roughly globular bivalve; its shell has two similar valves and pronounced ribs. When alive, the animal has two short fringed siphons which stick out from the open shell. Large white foot is kept at an angle inside shell when it is closed.

Cockles live buried quite near the surface of clean sand or mud, where sea birds can catch them for food. They feed by drawing in water through the lower siphon, filtering out the food particles, expelling water through the upper siphon.

They are found from midtide level to shallow offshore waters, usually where the tide runs rapidly and commonest in open sandy beaches. North Sea, Atlantic and Mediterranean. Often present in huge numbers. Also farmed in commercial beds.

The similar **Prickly Cockle** (1) has spiny ribs and a pink foot. It lives in sand and sandy mud in offshore waters of North Sea, Atlantic and Mediterranean. Empty shells are often washed ashore. Several other cockle species live in European waters.

OTHER BIVALVES

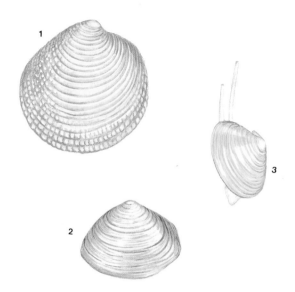

Venus Shells
have solid, rounded or oval
shells, often found on shores.
Valves similar, with beaks
turned inward & facing the
front. Animal has large foot &
two short siphons; burrows into
sand, on & off shore. Many
species live in N. Sea, Atlantic
& Med. **Warty Venus** (**1**) is
eaten in France.

Trough Shells (**2**)
have shells like equilateral
triangles. Valves are similar, the
beaks point forward & shells
often gape at the back. Empty
shells are often found on shores.
Live animals have two siphons

in a horny sheath & a wedge-
shaped, white foot. Several
species live in Med., Atlantic &
N. Sea, buried in sand or shell
gravel.

Tellins (**3**)
have smooth, flattened shells,
varying in shape but always
with a large external ligament.
Several species live in N. Sea,
Atlantic & Med., in sand or
mud of lower shore & offshore
waters. They have two very long
siphons; one siphon gropes
about on the surface for food.
Empty shells often found on
sandy beaches, the two valves
still joined.

97

OTHER BIVALVES

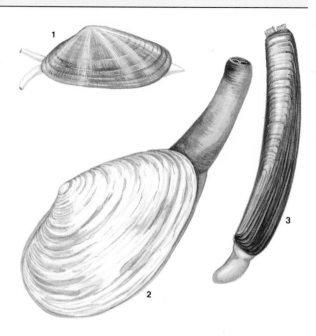

Wedge Shells (1)
have flattened, elongated shells,
very smooth & polished. Valves
of shell not equilateral; front
end larger than back. Live
animals have a similar life style
to Tellins. Many species occur
in N. Sea, Atlantic & Med.

Gapers
have large oval shells (up to
15cm long) that gape widely at
the back to reveal two huge,
fused siphons. Live animals live
buried vertically in stiff sand or
mud, siphons extended to the
surface to collect plankton.
Found in N. Sea, Atlantic &
Med. **Sand Gaper (2)** lives in
N. Sea & Atlantic; it is eaten in
N. America (where it is called a
soft-shelled clam).

Razor Shells
have long shells (up to 20cm
long), open at both ends.
Siphons short, projecting from
hind end; powerful foot projects
from the front. Live animals
live buried vertically in sand or
mud, from lower shore to
offshore waters. Several species
live in the N. Sea, Atlantic &
Med. **Curved Razor Shell (3)**
lives in clean sand at low tide
level.

BORING BIVALVES

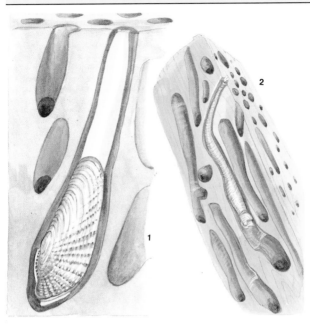

Piddocks

bore into rock or clay; the rock can resemble Emmenthal cheese. Their shells are hard, with fine teeth on the edge, used for boring. The shell is cut away at the front; the foot projects through the gap & grips the burrow. There is no hinge between the valves, only a ball & socket joint; & there are extra shell plates near the hinge. Siphons are long, joined together & half covered by a horny sheath. **Common Piddock** (1) lives in shale, chalk or wood on lower shores, from Ireland & southern Britain to the Med.

Shipworms (2)

bore into wood of old pilings & boats. The valves of their shells are much reduced & act as a drill; these valves are found at one end of the worm-like body. Animals bore long cylindrical tunnels into wood, soon reducing it to sawdust by the rotating action of the two valves. The burrow is lined by a calcareous lining, secreted by the shipworm. It is open at one end but can be closed by a pair of valves. Several species occur in Baltic, N. Sea, Atlantic & Med.

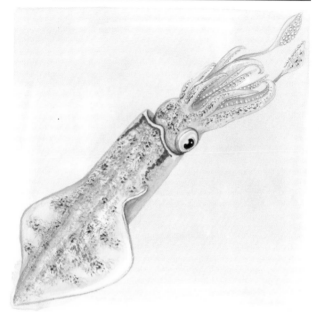

Torpedo-shaped molluscs with triangular fins. They have eight
tentacles around the mouth, all with rows of suckers, and two
longer arms with suckers only on their tips. Shell reduced to an
internal horny 'pen'. Mouth has a powerful beak.

Squid hunt smaller fishes. They avoid their own predators
(tunny, other fishes and whales) by propelling themselves
backwards, at the same time expelling black 'ink' to confuse the
predator. They can change colour almost instantaneously.

Squid swim in shoals in the open sea, from the coast of
Scandinavia southwards, in the Atlantic and North Sea to the
Mediterranean. Many are edible. They are caught commercially
in the Mediterranean and North Sea.

There are many squid species in European waters. They are all
similar in form. The males of **Northern Squid** (illustrated) grow
up to 60cm long, the females up to 35cm; they live in the open
waters of the Atlantic and North Sea.

A broad-bodied, shield-shaped mollusc with undulating fins. Usually striped in black and white, but changes of colour run across the body. Eight suckered tentacles and two long arms are held in front of it. Shell reduced to internal cuttlefish bone.

Cuttlefish hide, partly buried in sand by day, swimming slowly along and hunting by night for crabs, prawns and fishes. They can move quickly to catch their prey or shoot backwards to avoid predators. They also expel ink to confuse predators.

Cuttlefish are found in estuaries, sandy bays and in eelgrass beds along the Atlantic and North Sea coasts and in the Mediterranean. Cuttlefish bones are sold in pet shops and sometimes washed ashore.

Little Cuttle is the smallest European cuttlefish (only 2–5cm long). It has a rounded body and little fins like flaps on its sides. It lives over sandy seabeds in subtidal waters of the Atlantic and English Channel, changing colour with the sand.

101

An unmistakeable mollusc with a sac-like body, two large eyes, and eight tentacles in a webbed circle around the mouth. Each tentacle has a double row of suckers. Its warty skin changes colour to fit its background. Males are larger than females.

Hides by day in its lair among rocks, hunts at night for crabs, lobsters and fishes; can be a nuisance in lobster pots. If in danger it propels itself suddenly backwards. Females lay their eggs in rock crevices and guard them till they hatch.

Common in offshore waters from the English Channel to the Mediterranean; occasionally found on the lower shore. More common in summer in the northern part of its range. Edible. Caught commercially in the Mediterranean.

Little Octopus lives in subtidal waters off rocky shores, from the western Mediterranean north to Scandinavia and Iceland. It is small, only 50cm long at most, and has one row of suckers on each tentacle.

A burrowing worm with a smooth, soft, rounded body; it is thick in the middle, tapering at head and tail and with no distinct head. There are 13 pairs of red, feathery gills on the middle part of the body.

Lugworms live in U-shaped burrows with a depression at the front end, worm cast at the hind end. The burrow is lined with mucus. They feed like earthworms, swallowing sand, digesting the edible part and expelling the rest in the worm cast.

Found in sandy beaches and flats, from the Baltic and North Sea to the Atlantic, rarely in the Mediterranean, from midtide to subtidal levels. Their distinctive casts may be seen all over the beach when the tide goes out. Often dug up for bait.

Andouinia tentaculata also lives in burrows in muddy sand and gravel, under stones at low tide and subtidal levels in the Atlantic and North Sea. It grows up to 20cm long and has red, spirally twisted gills on most body segments.

103

A tube-forming worm. It has a short thorax of five segments, and a long abdomen with 300 small segments (normally concealed in the tube). The head bears two equal fans of feathery, banded tentacles, each arising from a fleshy lobe.

Peacock Worms live in smooth tubes, made of mud particles bound together by mucus. The worms emerge when the tide is in, extending their tentacles to trap small particles of food in the water. They can withdraw very suddenly if disturbed.

The tubes can be seen projecting above the surface of muddy sand and gravel at lowtide levels and in subtidal waters, from the North Sea to the Atlantic and Mediterranean.

One of the many Fan Worms in European waters. All live in tubes and have the double fan of tentacles. Some live in sand and gravel, others in horizontal tubes under kelp fronds, others in tubes wedged into cracks and crevices in rocks.

OTHER TUBE WORMS

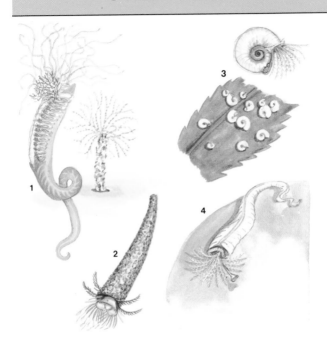

Sand Mason (1)
Tube up to 30cm long but embedded in sand for all but top 5cm; encrusted in sand & shell grains. Opening of tube divided into filaments. Worm has crown of writhing tentacles, with branched red gills behind the head. Lowtide & subtidal levels, N. Sea, Atlantic & Med.

***Pectinaria* worms (2)**
form little tubes like narrow cornets of sand grains. Found in sand of lower tide & subtidal levels; empty tubes often cast ashore. Baltic, N. Sea, Atlantic & Med.

***Spirorbis* worms (3)**
form small, hard, whitish tubes rolled in tight spirals like snail shells; tubes are only 3cm across at most. Abundant on rocks & stones, shells, seaweeds from mid to lower shore. Tentacles do not emerge unless worm is under water; & are rapidly withdrawn if disturbed. N. Sea, Atlantic & Med.

***Pomatoceros* worms (4)**
form irregular piles of hard, whitish, keeled tubes, up to 15cm long. Found on stones & shells on lower shore. N. Sea, Atlantic & Med.

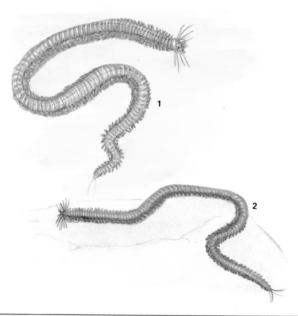

Large, active worms, their slightly flattened bodies formed of many segments. Each segment has a pair of bristly paddles, one on each side. Head has four eyes and several antennae. Can protrude a proboscis with a pair of black jaws from its mouth.

Ragworms are scavengers, feeding on the remains of dead animals and seaweeds. As spawning time approaches the hind end of the body develops large paddles, the animals emerge from their burrows and swim, all spawning together.

Many ragworms burrow in sand and mud, others crawl in rock pools or among seaweeds, from midtide levels of the shore to subtidal waters. Found from the Baltic and North Sea to Atlantic and Mediterranean. Often collected for bait.

Common Ragworm (1) and the larger King Ragworm (which can bite) burrow in sand and mud. Paddle-worms are similar to Ragworms but have large, leaf-like paddles and no jaws. **Green Paddle-worm** (2) lives among low tide rocks of many shores.

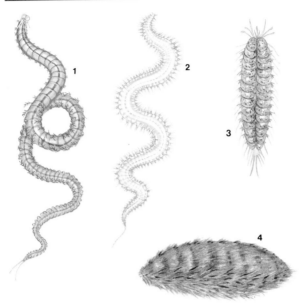

Red Rock-worm (1)
grows about 30cm long. Its
thick body has bunches of red
gills on each segment. Its head
has no antennae. Found in
gravelly sand, rock crevices &
kelp holdfasts. Lower shore &
subtidal waters of Med. &
Atlantic, north to English
Channel.

Catworm (2)
grows up to 25cm long. Its body
has a pearly sheen & its tail ends
in a long thread. Small head
lacks visible eyes or antennae.
An active worm living in sand
or gravel of mid & lower shores.
N. Sea, Baltic & Atlantic.

Scale Worm (3)
A small flattened worm,
generally up to 3cm long, with
two rows of overlapping,
kidney-shaped scales on its
back. Found under stones &
seaweeds on the lower shore.
One of several scale worms
found in the Baltic, N. Sea,
Atlantic & Med.

Sea-mouse (4)
Another scale worm, but in this
worm the scales are concealed
beneath fine grey hairs. Its
flanks are covered by iridescent
green & gold hairs. Found on
sandy seabeds in subtidal
waters. Baltic, N. Sea, Atlantic
& Med.

107

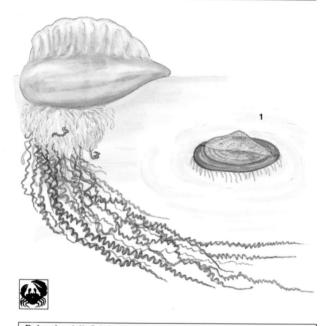

Related to jellyfish but with a gas-filled float which tapers at one end; float is pale blue sometimes tinged with pink, and has a deflatable crest. A complicated mass of tentacles hang down from the float; some contain powerful stinging cells.

This is not one animal, but a complex colony. Many kinds of individual animals live in the tentacles, some of them specialized for feeding, others defence (the ones with the stinging cells), others for reproduction.

Conspicuous. Found floating in the Mediterranean and Atlantic, sometimes cast up on western coasts of Europe, as far north as the British Isles. The toxic tentacles may trail up to 25 metres behind the float and are hazardous for swimmers.

By-the-wind-Sailor (1) has a flat, oval, bluish float with a stiff, diagonal sail and a fringe of stinging tentacles around the edge. It is only 12cm across. It lives in the open Atlantic and Mediterranean but may be cast ashore.

Jellyfish have soft, umbrella-shaped bodies and a fringe of tentacles around the rim of the umbrella. The mouth is on the underside and is bordered by four long, hanging, frilly flaps (arms). Both tentacles and arms contain stinging cells.

Jellyfish swim by opening and closing their umbrellas, their arms and tentacles trailing behind. They feed on small animals in the plankton. Young fishes may hide beneath the umbrellas.

Several different species are found in European waters. They drift, pulsing, in offshore waters and may be thrown up on the shore, dying or dead. Numbers vary enormously from year to year. They are found in seas and oceans worldwide.

Common Jellyfish (**1**) is often seen in docks and harbours. Its stinging cells seldom penetrate human skin. Even more harmless is ***Rhizostoma pulmo*** (**2**) which lacks tentacles. The large **Compass Jellyfish** (**3**) has long tentacles which do sting.

BEADLET ANEMONE
up to **7cm** across

Actinia equina

1

Smooth red, brown or green column is 'crowned' by five or six rings of sticky-feeling tentacles around a central mouth. About 200 tentacles altogether. There is a ring of blue spots around the outside of the tentacles.

These anemones remain contracted into jelly-like 'blobs' while the tide is out. The tentacles contain stinging cells which are used for catching prey (prawns, fishes etc.), also for stinging potential predators (and people).

They cling to crevices, rock overhangs and jetties, in pools, places hidden from bright light which do not dry out. Midshore to subtidal levels, on all kinds of coasts. North Sea, Atlantic and Mediterranean. The commonest anemone on British coasts.

Dahlia Anemone (1) is a broad, squat anemone (up to 12cm across) with short, banded tentacles; grains of sand or shell stick to the warts on its column. Found from midtide to subtidal waters in crevices and pools, under kelps and stones.

OTHER ANEMONES

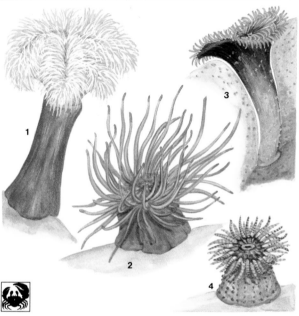

Plumose Anemone (1)
Large anemone, up to 12cm
tall. Column slimy, lobed at the
top, with fine tentacles. Colour
varies from pink to brown or
white. Found under rocks &
jetties, lower shore to subtidal
levels. N. Sea, Atlantic & Med.

Snakelocks Anemone (2)
A squat, flaccid anemone which
cannot close up. Usually green
or khaki, with about 100 wavy,
pink-tinged tentacles. Found in
shallow rock pools or on kelp
fronds, midshore to subtidal
levels. From Med. to west coast
of Scotland.

Daisy Anemone (3)
Trumpet-shaped column, up to
12cm tall. Up to 700 short
tentacles. Colour variable;
browns, pinks, creams. Found
on lower shore, in rock cracks &
pools, or sunk in muddy gravel,
its tentacles flush with the
surface. From Med. to west
coast of Scotland.

Gem Anemone (4)
Small anemone, only 3cm across
at most, with non-sticky warts
on column & about 50 stiff,
banded tentacles. Found in
crevices, on edges of rock pools,
mid to lower shore. From Med.
to Isle of Man.

SOFT CORALS

Dead Man's Fingers (1)
A colonial animal forming a
carpet of tough, rounded
'fingers', growing up to 25cm
high. Colour varies from white
to yellow, pink or red. Its tough
outer case houses many
individual animals (polyps),
each one like a tiny anemone.
When under water, the polyps
emerge from tiny holes all over
the colony; each has 8 feathery
tentacles. Found from lower
shore to subtidal waters on
shipwrecks, rocks, piers, kelp
fronds, often in strong currents.
From Bay of Biscay northwards,
in N. Sea & Atlantic.

Sea Fan (2)
Another colonial animal, this
one resembling an irregularly
branched fan up to 30cm tall;
mainly branched in one plane.
Usually pink but white fans also
occur. Tiny polyps, each with 8
tentacles, emerge from the
many knobs all over the fan.
Found in subtidal waters,
usually with the fan facing
across a current of water (so the
polyps can extract plankton
from the water). On rocks, from
the Med. north to the English
Channel.

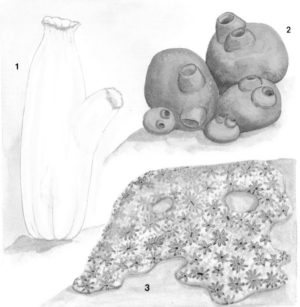

Simple bag-like animals living singly or in colonies. Each 'bag' has two openings or siphons. There are many species in European waters.

Common Sea-squirt (1)
forms single, soft, semi-transparent 'vases', each with two tubular siphons, one at the top & one on its side. It reaches 13cm tall when fully extended, but can close down if threatened. It expels a jet of water if squeezed. Found on rock overhangs & crevices, harbour walls & piers. Lower shore & subtidal waters. Atlantic, N. Sea & Med.

Gooseberry Sea-squirt (2)
Tough, compact, only 2cm tall, usually brick-red in colour. Individuals often found in large clusters, with their bases partly fused together. Lower shore & subtidal waters, in rock crevices, on kelp stalks. N. Sea & Atlantic, south to English Channel.

Star Sea-squirt (3)
Colonial animal, with star-shaped clusters of individuals embedded in a thick, gelatinous base. Midshore to subtidal waters, encrusting rocks, stones & seaweeds. N. Sea, Atlantic, Med.

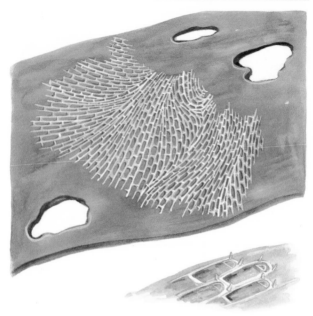

This sea-mat forms flat white, honeycomb-like patches on kelps and wracks, irregular in shape. Formed of many delicate rectangular compartments. Two of the corners of each compartment bear single blunt white spines.

When covered with water, each compartment can be seen to contain an individual animal. It extends a ring of tentacles to trap food particles. Sea-slugs and sea-spiders often graze on sea mats.

This sea mat is abundant on kelps and wracks from midshore to subtidal waters. Found around the coasts of the North Sea, Atlantic and Mediterranean.

This is one of several flat sea mats found on seaweeds. Other species resemble gelatinous sponges, lobed fronds or tufted corals. All have the same compartmentalized structure. They may be found on rocks as well as seaweeds.

Porifera

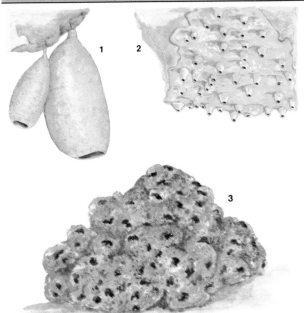

Sponges are simple animals, generally with numerous openings (through which water is drawn in) and one or few larger openings (through which water is expelled). There are many species on the lower shore & in subtidal waters all around European coasts.

Purse Sponges look like little vases; they may be solitary or form connected groups. Groups of the purse sponges known as *Grantia compressa* (1) hang from rock overhangs, often among red seaweeds on the lower shore. Med., Atlantic & N. Sea.

Encrusting sponges form tough patches on rock overhangs & in crevices, on kelps, shells etc., Different species may be red, orange, green, yellow, blue or grey. They may form small discrete patches or spread irregularly, like the **Breadcrumb Sponge** (2). This is a common species, found on the lower shore & in subtidal waters of the Baltic, N. Sea, Atlantic & Med.

Bath Sponge (3) is found on rocks in shallow waters of the Med. Its cleaned skeletons form the natural bath sponges of commerce.

115

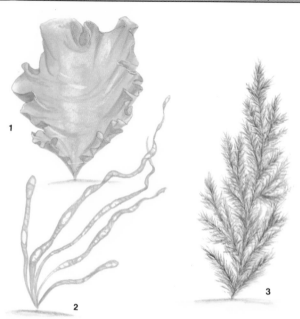

Frond-like plants, mostly found high up on the shore or where a stream runs into the sea. Distinguished by their bright green colour from other seaweeds.

Sea Lettuce (1)

resembles soft, translucent lettuce, with bunches of irregularly-lobed fronds, 12–25cm long, growing from a basal stalk. Older fronds may turn white on the margins. It grows on rocks & stones (not in pools), especially where there is fresh water, on all levels of the shore. Baltic, N. Sea, Atlantic & Med.

Enteromorpha intestinalis (2)

forms unbranched, hollow green tubes, up to 30cm long, often partly filled with air & bleached by the sun. Mainly found where fresh water runs into the sea, salt marshes, estuaries, mud flats, pools at high tide level. Baltic, N. Sea, Atlantic & Med.

Cladophora rupestris (3)

forms much-branched, wiry, dark green tufts up to 12cm tall. Found on rocks from midshore to subtidal waters, especially under wracks. Baltic, N. Sea, Atlantic & Med.

Laminariaceae

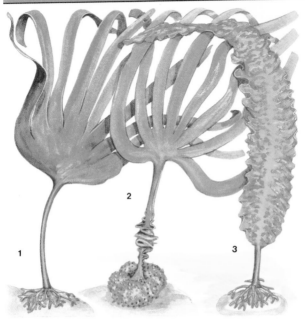

Brown seaweeds with massive, leathery fronds, 1m or more long, & thick stalks attached to rocks by a root-like holdfast. Grow on lower shore & in subtidal waters.

Oarweed (1)

has a flexible, smooth stalk, & a broad blade up to 2m long, divided into flat fingers. Holdfast is much-branched, its 'roots' gripping the rocks. Abundant on lower shores of Baltic, N. Sea & Atlantic, south to English Channel. Forest Kelp is also very common & very similar but has a stiff, rough stalk.

Furbelows (2)

has a bulbous, warty, hollow holdfast. Stalk flat, with wavy frills at the base. Blade massive & fan-shaped, often 2m long, with long flat fingers. Found among other kelps at extreme low tide & into water 20m deep. N. Sea & Atlantic, south to English Channel.

Sugar Kelp (3)

has undivided, undulating, wavy-edged fronds, 3m or more long. Attached to rocks & stones on muddy or sandy flats from lower shore to about 20m deep. N. Sea & Atlantic, south to English Channel. Edible.

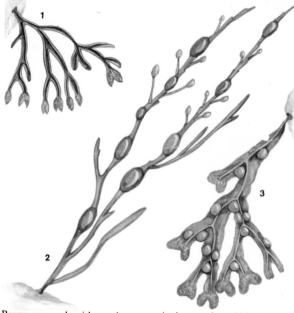

Brown seaweeds with tough, leathery, strip-like, forked fronds & disc-like holdfasts. They grow in distinct, obvious zones on rocks of upper & middle shores.

Channel Wrack (1)
forms branched, grooved fronds, up to 15cm long, often with swollen, granular tips; they turn brittle & black as they dry. Common on rocks at high tide & in splash zone; N. Sea & Atlantic.

Knotted Wrack (2)
forms much-branched, flat fronds, up to 1m long, with

single, egg-shaped bladders in the middle of the blade but no midrib; more olive-green than brown & turns green-black as it dries. Only common on sheltered rocky shores & in estuaries; then often covering rocks of upper & middle shore. N. Sea & Atlantic.

Bladder Wrack (3)
has wavy-edged, branched fronds, up to 90cm long; with distinct midribs & bladders (often in pairs) on either side of midrib. Tips of fronds often swollen & granular. Abundant on mid shore rocks. N. Sea & Atlantic.

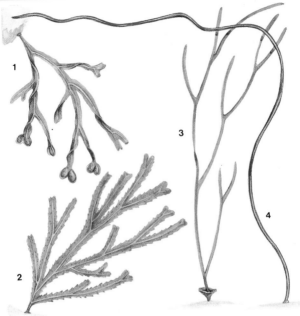

Spiral Wrack (1)

has broad, flat, branched fronds up to 40cm long. They have a distinct midrib & no bladders, grow with a partial twist & may have swollen, granular tips. Forms a zone beneath Channel Wrack on all but very exposed shores; N. Sea & Atlantic.

Serrated Wrack (2)

has broad, flat, much-branched fronds up to 60cm long. They have serrated edges, distinct midrib & no bladders. Common on rocks of lower middle shore, just above kelps. Baltic, N. Sea & Atlantic.

Thongweed (3)

has a toadstool-like holdfast with a concave top; from its centre grow strap-shaped, branched 'thongs', usually about 1m long. Grows in rock pools, on rocks of lower shore & subtidal levels; Atlantic coasts & English Channel.

Bootlace Weed (4)

has long, slimy, unbranched 'bootlaces' up to 6m long. Young fronds are attached to rocks, from lower shore to 20m deep, but are often torn loose & seen on beaches or floating in summer. Baltic, N. Sea & Atlantic.

119

RED SEAWEEDS

Rhodophyceae

Red or reddish-brown seaweeds, very variable in form. They cannot stand drying or bright light. On shore they grow in pools or at lower tide levels, often under wracks & kelps.

Dulse (1)
has tough, dark red, blade-like fronds, often with distinct lobes near the base. Grows on brown seaweeds & rocks from mid shore to subtidal waters. N. Sea & Atlantic. Edible.

Laver Bread (2)
has membranous, dark red-purple fronds up to 20cm long. Grows on rocks & stones of exposed shores & beaches. N. Sea, Atlantic & Med. Edible.

Carragheen (3)
is very variable in form. Usually has wide, flat, much-divided, dark red fronds. Attached to rocks from mid shore to subtidal levels. N. Sea & Atlantic. Edible.

***Delesseria sanguinea* (4)**
has deep pink, wavy-edged, leaf-like fronds up to 25cm long. Grows on rocks or kelps in deep, shady pools of the lower shore & into subtidal waters. N. Sea & Atlantic.

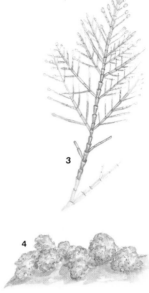

Lomentaria articulata (**1**)
has hollow, gelatinous fronds,
like a string of beads with
branches at the constrictions.
Grows on rocks & other
seaweeds in pools; mid & lower
shore. N. Sea & Atlantic.

Pepper Dulse (**2**)
has tough, branched fronds with
finger-like divisions at sides &
tips. Varies from yellow-green
to red-purple, larger & darker
(up to 20cm tall) in less exposed
places. Grows on rocks & in
pools from mid shore to subtidal
levels. N. Sea, Atlantic & Med.
Has distinctive smell & taste.

Coralweed (**3**)
is stiff & brittle, with dull pink
or purple, branched tufts, up to
12cm tall. It forms a fringe just
below the water line of rock
pools. Very common on mid
shore of N. Sea & Atlantic.

Lithothamnion species (**4**) form
hard, pink, knobbly crusts on
rocks in pools of mid & lower
shore in the N. Sea, Atlantic &
Med. *Lithophyllum* species are
similar but form flat crusts.
Both forms may cover large
areas; they are hardly
recognizable as seaweeds.

Index and Checklist

Keep a record of your sightings by inserting a tick in the box

Glossary

Continental Shelf. A submerged shelf that surrounds the
continents. It slopes gradually to a depth of about 200m, then falls
away more steeply down the continental slope to the abyss. The
continental shelf underlies the Baltic and North Seas, and
surrounds the British Isles; but is only about 10–50km wide in
the Atlantic from the Bay of Biscay south, and in the
Mediterranean.

Eelgrass. A marine grass that grows in eelgrass beds, on fine sand
or mud from lowtide level to a depth of about 4m.

Gills. 'Breathing' organs of an aquatic animal. They are on each
side of the throat in a fish, suspended on bony arches (the gill
arches).

Gill rakers. Projections on the gill arches of a fish; often used to
collect planktonic food in water passing over the gills.

Gill slit. Opening behind the head of a fish, connecting the throat
to the outside.

Hydroid. Small colonial animal related to sea anemones. It forms
tufts on rocks and seaweeds.

Keeled. Having a sharp median ridge.

Mantle. In molluscs — a fold of skin that covers the body and
secretes the shell. It lines the shell in bivalves.

Offshore Waters. Coastal waters.

Parasite. Organism that lives in or on another living organism (its
host) and feeds on the host, usually without killing it.

Pelagic. An animal that lives in the open sea (in contrast to one that
lives on the bottom).

Plankton (adj. planktonic). Small animals and plants that drift in
the currents of the sea.

Siphon. A tube that directs a current of water.

Spiracle. The first gill-slit of sharks and rays (usually smaller than
the others).

Illustrated Glossary

Crustacean

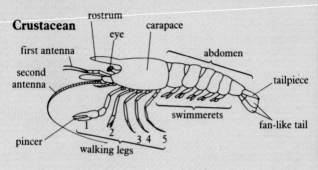

rostrum
eye
carapace
first antenna
abdomen
second antenna
tailpiece
pincer
fan-like tail
swimmerets
1 2 3 4 5
walking legs

Starfish

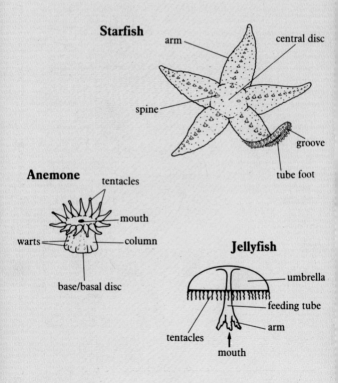

arm
central disc
spine
groove
tube foot

Anemone

tentacles
mouth
warts
column
base/basal disc

Jellyfish

umbrella
feeding tube
arm
tentacles
mouth